They Arrived in an MMMBop!

It's all here! Learn what their lives were like, growing up in Oklahoma and traveling the world . . . how they were influenced by their parents' music . . . how they paid their dues, performing at birthday parties, school assemblies, state fairs and music festivals—even performing in the parking lots of clubs they were too young to get into!

Find out what life behind the scenes is like, at concerts and on the road. Do they get along? Where do they get their inspiration? How do they write their songs? Where—and how—can you meet them? Who's the perfect Hanson for you? Get all the info on the teen scene's newest stars . . .

Hanson!

Look for Other Biographies from Archway Paperbacks

hanson
MMMBop to the Top

an unauthorized biography

jill matthews

AN ARCHWAY PAPERBACK
Published by POCKET BOOKS
New York London Toronto Sydney Tokyo Singapore

AN ARCHWAY PAPERBACK *Original*

 An Archway Paperback published by
POCKET BOOKS, a division of Simon & Schuster Inc.
1230 Avenue of the Americas, New York, NY 10020

Copyright © 1997 by Jill Matthews
Cover photo © Anthony Cutajar

ISBN: 0-671-02490-6

First Archway Paperback printing September 1997

19 18 17 16

AN ARCHWAY PAPERBACK and colophon are registered trademarks of Simon & Schuster Inc.

Printed in the U.S.A.

IL 5+

For Hanson fans everywhere: finally, a band of your own. You believed. And you were right.

Contents

Introduction

All it took was an "MMMBop"—a unit of time measured in the amount of time it takes to snap your fingers—and *poof!* From the "middle of nowhere" out sprung Hanson: Isaac, Taylor and Zachary, totally talented, awesomely adorable teen brothers to set music charts and young female hearts on fire.

The trio of Tulsa towheads took the music world completely by surprise. No one was prepared for the instant mega-popularity of their single, the debut album—and the brothers themselves.

How'd they really get so far, so fast? It took, of course, much more than a ditty named "MMMBop," and way longer than a finger-snapping microsecond to reach number one. The song refers to "the secret no one knows." What's Hanson's secret to success?

No secret at all. What it really took was . . . only everything: a whole lot of grit, determination, talent and support. For Hanson is that rare band that grew organically. In the best tradition of grassroots America, their success came by evolution, not revolution. It came without benefit of Hollywood hype, without any adult master crafter pulling the strings and directing them to sing. Brothers Isaac, Taylor and Zac did it themselves: *They* write the songs, *they* play their instruments, *they* create and nurture their signature heavenly harmonies.

Most of all, Hanson's success took faith. When no one else believed in them, when rejections came by the bushelfull, when professionals were told it would ruin their careers to represent Hanson, still Ike, Taylor and Zac believed—in their music, in themselves. It took five years, but now millions of fans the world over believe too.

What those fans don't know, however, is . . . only everything: What's the real story behind Isaac, Taylor and Zachary Hanson? What are the boys really like? *That's* the secret no one knows. Everyone will, beginning now.

hanson

MMMBop to the Top

BEGINNINGS

The grin on Taylor Hanson's flushed face stretched from ear to ear. He couldn't hear a word anyone was saying—let alone what he or his brothers were about to sing—but he didn't care. The deafening screams of joy coming from the sea of rapturous faces around him told him all he needed to know. The homemade banners—"I ♥ Hanson" and "Hanson Rules"—were icing on the cake. What a rush!

Standing at the microphone, tambourine in hand, he took a deep breath and glanced at his brothers on either side of him. Ike, guitar strapped on, and Zac, castanets in each hand, were clearly feeling what he was feeling: This was their moment, a moment they'd worked long and hard for but had never anticipated would come quite this soon. As the trio launched into "MMMBop," the screams got louder, and try as he might, Taylor still couldn't stop smiling. Every girl in the place who wasn't screaming was singing and bopping along. They seemed to know every word by heart.

Later, Tay would joke, "It was nuts! I couldn't hear myself. It was the worst performance we *ever* played!"

Musically, maybe. In every other way, it was one of the best. For that was the scene at Paramus Park Mall in New Jersey. It was just after "MMMBop" had been released, before *Middle of Nowhere* had even come out. Originally, Hanson was supposed to sing two songs and field a question-and-answer session for the fans they hoped would show up. They figured that maybe a few hundred kids would come; after all, they weren't really *that* well known yet.

They figured wrong. It was estimated that upwards of six thousand over-the-top Hanson fans clogged the entire mall; several thousand showed up eight hours early, just to get a good spot near the band. It was by far the hugest, most deliriously enthusiastic crowd Hanson had ever encountered. The band never even got to do the interview: The fan frenzy was just too fevered and overwhelming. For the first time in their lives, the boys actually needed a phalanx of bodyguards to spirit them in and out of the mall safely.

That first time marked the official beginning of Hanson-mania—the first time the boys realized what a long way they'd come from their own beginnings!

* * *

The Hanson story begins, not exactly in the middle of nowhere, but close. Middle of America is more like it. Tulsa, Oklahoma's second-largest city, sits pretty much right in the middle of the USA. Bisected by the Arkansas River, it's home to an eclectic mix of the old—lots of Wild West memorabilia—and the new: A thriving music and arts scene dominates a downtown area.

Musically, it is mostly attuned to the country scene—megastars like Garth Brooks and Bryan White hail from Oklahoma—but Tulsa prides itself on being a hotbed of cutting-edge jazz, classic rock, and Cajun blues as well. Until Hanson, the pop scene had not been terribly well represented—but that's getting ahead of our story.

Tulsa is proudly multi-culti to the max, boasting sizable communities of all types of Americans, from Native to African, Christian to Jewish, Asian to Indian. Other minorities are represented as well. The city is very much a diverse melting pot. Children growing up there naturally learn to accept and appreciate each other's differences. Although some parts of town are clearly more affluent than others, it has come a long way since the socs and greasers fought it out in the Tulsa of S.E. Hinton's *The Outsiders,* the most famous book ever set there. (The author, who also wrote *Tex* and *Rumblefish,* still lives there, in fact.)

Tulsa's geography is as divergent as its population. Parts of the city are mountainous and rural; some areas are tractlike and suburban—the part where the Hansons live is somewhere in between those two;

other parts are citified and congested. Its landmark, a monumental statue of the Golden Driller, symbolizes Tulsa's biggest industry: petroleum.

Isaac, Taylor and Zachary Hanson are very much a product of their mid-America hometown. They're not slick, Hollywood kids, but rather open, unaffected, boy-next-door boys. Which doesn't mean they're provincial country bumpkins: They are smart, savvy and fortunate in having been exposed to a wide range of influences—historical, cultural and societal. They've met and become friends with many different types of people from all walks of life.

Hanson family roots go deep in Tulsa. The boys' parents, Walker and Diana, were born and lived their entire lives there. Grandparents, aunts, uncles and cousins still live there; further, the family counts hundreds of hometown folks as friends. Talk to anyone in Tulsa: The Hansons are well known, well respected and sincerely beloved. And, as friends and associates often add, "They have deep faith and are very family oriented. No one deserves success more than they do."

Growing up, both Walker and Diana, who attended the same high school, were very involved in music. Although Diana was a music major in college and Walker played guitar, neither seriously considered music as a future profession. Mostly it was an avocation for which they displayed above-average aptitude and which just brought them a lot of joy.

It wasn't just singing, either. "When my parents were in high school, they were really into the arts scene," Isaac explains. "They did lots of plays."

Taylor adds, "They sang and acted and, later on, were actually in a gospel group." That group, the Horizons, traveled extensively and performed in churches throughout the country, spreading the joy of music wherever they could. The goal, however, was never to go pro, and they never did.

When Walker and Diana got married, they settled into a rambling home in West Tulsa, a quiet neighborhood separated from the downtown area by the Arkansas River and several industrial parks. Walker began his career in Tulsa's biggest industry: He became an accountant for an oil-drilling company. From the get-go, he and his wife knew that the job might entail a good bit of travel, since offshore drilling was a huge part of the company's business. They knew they might even have to live in foreign countries for stretches of time. The couple saw that as exciting and challenging. It's doubtful they ever considered a potentially peripatetic lifestyle as a detriment to their dream of starting a family. Wherever life took them, they'd go together. That was the plan. Somehow, they'd figure out a way to make kids and schooling fit into it.

On November 17, 1980, their first child was born. A blond, brown-eyed bundle of boy-joy, they christened him Clarke Isaac; from the start, he was known as Ike.

Less than two and a half years later, on March 14, 1983, the Hansons were blessed with another child. Blue-eyed and blond-haired, this one was named Jordan Taylor, soon tagged Tay.

October 22, 1985, brought the family their third

look-alike son, the caramel-eyed Zachary Walker; everyone immediately called him Zac.

The boys' earliest memories involve two things: the closeness they shared and the music that surrounded them in their formative years. "There was always singing and music around the house," Ike has said. "My mom's been singing and listening to a lot of music ever since I can remember."

It wasn't just Mom. Dad too would join in, and not only on what the radio played. Both had a knack for making up original ditties and would sing them together. The kind of music their parents exposed the Hanson brothers to was a mix: While some was gospel, a lot was not. As Taylor has told it, "Our mom really liked Billy Joel. And she'd say, 'Here guys, listen to this.' One of the first songs we sang was 'For the Longest Time.'"

One of the first songs they learned to sing—make that *learned to harmonize on*—however, was the one they routinely sang after saying grace at each meal; the dinner blessing, "Amen."

"When we were younger, we sang at the dinner table," Isaac explains. "One day our dad taught us two-part harmony on 'Amen.' Which soon led to three-part harmony when Zac was old enough to join in."

To no one's surprise, the Hanson brothers had beautiful voices. The special harmony that can only come from being brothers was there from the get-go. But just being good at something doesn't automatically mean you like doing it. In this case, however, all three brothers instantly loved the way they sounded together.

"It was the most natural thing in the world for us to sing together," Isaac asserts.

And once they'd learned that three-part harmony, there was no stopping them. Making music became their primary "play" activity. Without prodding, they spent more time at it than in front of the TV set, video-game monitor, practicing karate on each other, or even outside on their bikes. In no time, Isaac, Taylor and Zac were working up their own versions of songs, both from their Christian music backgrounds and from what they heard on Top 40 radio. And soon after that, following in their parents' musical footsteps, the three little boys began composing their own original ditties.

They loved what they were doing, so they just kept doing it. Because they just kept doing it, they just got better at it. Soon those three-part harmonies were supertight, and soon they had a little compendium of Hanson originals. None of these were yet full-out songs; after all, the boys were really little and as yet had had no real musical education. But the seeds of what would become the Hanson sound were being planted. As they'd later write in "MMMBop," a lot of planting ensued, although they surely couldn't have known way back then which seeds would take root and grow. And how big!

Not unexpectedly, in the late 1980s, Walker Hanson, who'd risen through the ranks to become director of international accounting, was informed that his job with the oil-drilling company was about to take him out of the country. The family wasn't unprepared; they'd known this day would come. There was never a question that they wouldn't go together. Walker and Diana explained to their boys that they'd be spending the next year in several new homes in the South American countries of Ecuador and Venezuela, as well as Trinidad and Tobago in the Caribbean. They'd be meeting many different kinds of people. It was presented as a wonderful opportunity.

So that the boys' education would not be disrupted, Diana had already decided to home-school her brood. In other words, Ike, Taylor and Zac did not join the neighborhood kids and get on the school bus. Instead, large chunks of time were set aside every day for their lessons, with Mom as the teacher, in all academic subjects. It meant a huge responsibility and total dedication by Diana to the children. College-educated and deeply committed, she was prepared.

Home-schooling means different things in different states. It's fairly common in Oklahoma, where, according to journalist Thomas Conner, "Some people choose it for religious reasons. They want to 'protect' their kids from certain influences that they might be exposed to in public schools." Other people choose home-schooling simply because they're not satisfied with the quality of education in their local school system and perhaps can't afford private-school tuition. "Home-schooling is getting very prevalent out here," says a Tulsa father of two.

Tulsa Public Schools spokesperson Gary Lytal explains the system: "Parents do it all. They don't have any help or assistance from the public schools at all. There is no [formal] testing. But if a child wants to go on to vocational school or college after being home-schooled, of course he or she would take the appropriate tests, the GED, ACT or SAT."

Home-schooling is clearly not for everyone, but for the Hansons—who have not stated publicly why *they* chose the method—it was the perfect way to stay together as a family on the move and control the quality of their children's education at the same time.

As they prepared for the big move overseas, naturally, they didn't neglect their beloved music. Because of language and cultural differences in South America and the Caribbean, the family knew they would not be able to tune in to their favorite Top 40 radio station. Nor would they be able to watch television: There wasn't any! They realized that the only way they'd be able to hear what they liked was BYOM: Bring Your Own Music. So they did.

Isaac divulges that they didn't give a whole lot of thought to the music they brought with them. At the time, they had no clue how much it would influence them. As the oldest Hanson bro explained to *Tulsa World* magazine: "Before we left, we bought a bunch of tapes, the Time/Life compilation series of old '50s and '60s rock 'n' roll—everything from 1957–1969. We had no radio to listen to and it was just a coincidence that we picked this particular style to take with us. But it was very inspirational. It's just great music, all that Chuck Berry, Bobby Darin, Otis Redding, Aretha Franklin, old Beatles. These people are the origins for what all music is today. They're the ones who started it all. We love that kind of music."

Taylor added, "That's the music that inspired us the most."

The Hanson brothers ended up listening to that music over and over. They still know every word to songs like "Johnny B. Goode," "Splish Splash," "Rockin' Robin" and "Good Golly Miss Molly." Those tapes became not only a crash course in the history of old-time rock 'n' roll, but the foundation for the exact kind of music Hanson would end up doing themselves many years later.

The taped music was reinforced as their parents led family sing-alongs each night. As their dad told a magazine reporter, "The boys really started singing when we went overseas. At night, I would get the guitar and play for them for half an hour."

Life overseas was not without its challenges, joys and difficulties. Along with other families from their dad's company, the Hansons lived in a company-run compound or "camp," as it was called. Some camps were practically in the middle of the jungle and utterly lacking in what Americans think of as normal stuff. Aside from no TV or radio, there were also no cars, malls, or sports stores, and the food took a lot of getting used to. So did the bugs, frogs, bats and rats!

Of course, there were some cool things too. Like

getting to swim every day in countries where it was summer all year 'round. That was quite a change from Tulsa, which routinely gets several feet of snow each winter. And like getting to see six-foot-long iguanas, wild parrots flying around and shining lights in the faces of the crocodiles in the lagoon at night. It was an adventurous life for the three active, inquisitive Hanson boys.

Best of all was the sense of community and closeness being strangers in these strange lands afforded the family. They became fast pals with the other Oklahoma families in the oil company's compound. "The kids were free to run around," remembers a family friend, "everybody looked after everybody else. The pace was slower, it was tranquil, they got in touch with the great outdoors and with nature, and there was no commercialism. It was like stepping back in time." And because there were fewer distractions, the Hanson family, already close-knit, came to rely on and appreciate each other more than ever.

Even though they only lived in South America and the Caribbean for one short year, their experiences clearly made a huge impact on Ike, Taylor and Zac. Perhaps it accounts, at least in part, for their lack of interest in fads and material things like trendy clothes or designer labels. They didn't miss what they didn't have. They just ended up focusing on what they did have: lots of freedom, lots of love and lots of music.

THE A CAPPELLA YEARS

The memories of their time abroad stayed with them long after the family returned to Tulsa to resume their normal lives. By 1989, when they came back home, Ike, Taylor and Zac had a new little sister: Jessica was born in 1988. She'd be joined by another little girl in 1991, named Avery. The littlest Hanson, brother Mac, didn't come along until 1994. The household was a noisy, busy one.

Although forming a band was the perfect family project for the Hanson brothers, according to Taylor, there was no "one moment in time" when he and his brothers suddenly decided to go pro. "I think it was a natural progression, just because we were always singing." Taylor's totally on the mark: Hanson really did take it step by step. In very small steps.

The singing led to harmonizing, and the harmonizing led to writing original songs. "We didn't even

12

think about it, it just happened," Taylor says with a shrug.

It happened a lot. Especially when their parents would go out at night, leaving explicit instructions for Ike, Taylor and Zac to get the chores done—wash the dishes and vacuum the carpet—by the time they came home. Inevitably, Walker and Diana Hanson would return to a sink full of dirty dishes and a carpet that still needed vacuuming. The boys hadn't been lazy. "Instead of doing our chores, we usually spent the time writing a new song," Zac explains.

While most parents might have been annoyed, the Hansons were not. Instead, as Zac tells it, "They'd say, 'This better be good,' and give us a chance to sing it. Then—of course—we'd still have to do the dishes!"

It's doubtful Hanson will ever record those nascent musical efforts. The boys probably don't even remember most of them. "At first," Ike admits, "we didn't even write 'em out. We just sang 'em."

Taylor adds, "We'd just have them in our heads."

Ike didn't start writing his lyrics on paper until he entered third grade. "Rain Falling Down" is the name of that first official Hanson song ever written.

Writing the music to go with those lyrics didn't get accomplished until Ike began what would be five years of formal classical piano lessons. They weren't taken to further any future career plan. Diana Hanson just believed that music education should go hand in hand with the academics she was teaching them. Taylor and Zac soon followed suit, taking piano lessons as well. Unsurprisingly, all three boys took to the instrument naturally. Taylor, the most natural of all, picked it up quickest.

In spite of all the talent, the time spent composing music, the encouragement of their parents and their obvious love for it, until the very end of 1991, neither Ike, Taylor or Zac really thought about performing—not outside the confines of their own home, that is. All that changed, for all three of them, during their dad's office Christmas party in 1991.

The company Walker Hanson works for prides itself on being very family-oriented. They sponsor many events such as Easter egg hunts, picnics, Christmas parties and other functions designed for the families of their employees.

At that holiday party—and no one remembers why, exactly—Ike, Taylor and Zac, all of eleven, eight and six years old, respectively, suddenly decided to get up in front of everyone for an impromptu performance. They hadn't specifically practiced for it, and they had no instruments. But the boys just lined up, snapped their fingers and began harmonizing on a few of the rock 'n' roll oldies they'd learned so well during their time abroad. In no time, everyone at the party began to snap their fingers, tap their toes and clap along with the boys. And that's how it happened: The enthusiastic appreciation from that audience fueled the Hansons' desire to do more.

As their proud father later told a magazine, "That [unrehearsed performance] really got their juices going."

Taylor concurs. Although they still didn't have a

career plan, and indeed were far from dreaming of being on MTV with a number-one single, they did come to a joint realization after that Christmas party. "We just wanted to sing in front of crowds."

In 1992 they started to do just that.

With their parents solidly behind them, Ike, Taylor and Zac dubbed themselves the Hanson Brothers, and began working up an act. Because their skills on the piano were still rudimentary, and they didn't play other instruments yet, the boys stuck with their strong suit: harmony. The Hanson Brothers would perform *a cappella* (with no musical accompaniment) versions of their favorite oldies, sprinkled with a few Hanson originals. Ike remembers the songs exactly. "The first music we ever performed were '50s and '60s songs like 'Johnny B. Goode,' 'Splish Splash' and 'Rockin' Robin.'"

The boys voted in favor of dressing exactly alike for their gigs. Which doesn't mean Mom went out and bought them new clothes. The Hanson Brothers' earliest stage outfits came straight from their closet: blue jeans (Zac's rolled up!), sneakers and white T-shirts under unbuttoned denim jackets. Matching crew cuts and sunglasses completed the "tough tyke" look.

With a musical repertoire and a look all set, they made themselves available to perform wherever they could. Which basically meant word-of-mouth advertising.

Not surprisingly, word of mouth got them gigs on a very small, very local scale for which they rarely got paid—but one gig always led to another. Hanson now seems too young to have ever paid its dues, but the Hanson Brothers surely did, singing at such low-glam events as family reunions, office parties and their neighbors' backyard barbecues. No matter how small their audience, however, or how dippy the venue, Ike, Taylor and Zac always gave their all. And from the get-go, they clearly had something special. They were never just the neighbor boys do-wopping on a lark.

A friend remembers: "They were invited to sing at my girlfriend's party, and they just came in and blew everyone's minds, these three little kids, singing great harmonies." That particular party led to an invitation to sing at halftime during the NAIA Men's National Basketball Championship (held annually in Tulsa), where again they were greeted with enthusiastic applause.

Audience appreciation and their own ever-growing love and talent for music naturally took Ike, Taylor and Zac to the next step: playing outside their own neighborhood, for people they didn't know. They took that step in May 1992, at Mayfest, a popular week-long arts, crafts and music festival held in downtown Tulsa. "It's the biggest kickoff-to-summer event we have," says an organizer. To prepare, Isaac, Taylor and Zac rehearsed four hours a day, five days a week, for a month!

Mayfest traditionally draws artists of all stripes and levels. Indeed, it has become a common stop on the way up for many stars. The Fabulous Thunderbirds, Jonny Lang, Taylor Dayne and Eddie Money have all played there in recent seasons. Of course, the more famous folks play on the larger stages. When the Hanson Brothers signed up, organizers had just instituted a "community stage." The idea was to showcase local talent and have a competition, where audiences would vote on the twenty-five best local acts of the year. Those would be invited to play again the following year. It was far from high-glam. As one cynic described it, "Anyone who wanted to play, could. People who play the community stage at Mayfest would play for free at a car wreck."

Indeed, Mayfest had no budget to actually pay community stage performers, but at that point, Ike, Taylor and Zac weren't in it for the money. They weren't even looking to make a career out of their music. They just loved to perform, much as their own parents had done in their youth.

And perform the boys did—memorably, if not brilliantly—that year at Mayfest. The Hanson Brothers were on stage for close to an hour, doing a fifteen-song set. As their dad later remarked to a reporter, "Isaac and Taylor really worked off each other well, and Zac picked up the rhythm. Of their fifteen songs, six were original Hanson compositions." Nevertheless, they didn't top the competition that year. Which didn't bother them: One observer remembers little Zac, oblivious to the contest, zooming off on his skateboard right after the show.

Tulsa World reporter Thomas Conner observes, "They got up and did some do-wop, soul and R 'n' B covers, some Aretha Franklin is what I recall. It was all *a cappella,* not even a backing tape. They just harmonized and everybody just said, 'Aren't they cute?' "

That pretty much sums up the attitude of their hometown neighbors for the next several years. As Thomas Conner relates, "No one ever thought of them as a professional band or anything. They were just 'the little Hanson Brothers' who'd show up at Mayfest and sing at a church or two, that's it. The reaction to them was always, 'Oh, aren't they cute, the harmonies are fantastic and they really sound good, but so what?' No one ever thought, 'Wow, they're really going to go places.' "

No one but their parents and the boys themselves, that is. For as the years went on, Ike, Taylor and Zac's feelings about what they were doing changed ever so slightly. They still loved it—more than ever, in fact; but at some point—again, no one can say exactly when—the Hansons' beloved hobby became more than a just-for-the-fun-of-it family project. It was slowly evolving into a dream to record their music and eventually get signed by a major record label. Translation: Sometime between 1992 and 1995, Ike, Taylor and Zac decided they wanted to get famous!

Their parents were behind them, but cautiously. "We're just going to set them up, let them go and see what happens," Walker Hanson explained to a magazine reporter. "This has all been so fun, we're just going with it."

Going with it meant working even harder than before, as well as making some changes. First, they refined their act. Ike explains: "We're very vocal-oriented, so we were always going to stay with that, but we switched from just standing there, snapping our fingers and harmonizing, to more of an R 'n' B thing. We wanted to do a Boyz II Men/New Edition type thing. So we added dancing. Back then we weren't playing instruments, so we got to be more involved with the audience, coaxing them to dance and clap along with us, that sort of thing."

They did add occasional instrumentation and singing to a backing track; when possible, Ike or Taylor would play piano.

The brothers also rethought their all-matching look. "Originally," Taylor says, "if we didn't match exactly, we'd at least be color-coordinated. But eventually we kind of said, 'This is a little corny.'" They also ditched the crew cuts. When they look back now, all three might be forgiven if they wince at their next attempt at coordinating hairdos. As reported by *Urban Tulsa* magazine, the Hanson Brothers circa 1994 had pageboy haircuts (!) and wore "semi-hip-hop" clothing. In another incarnation, they admit to wearing their hair shaved in the back and longer on top—that old wedge look.

The main thing they did, however, was take their act on the road, as far away as they could, as often as they could. Because the boys were home-schooled, there was never a problem with missing classes: Classes went where they did. And though Zac now jokes that "our parents forced us into this," the truth is that because their parents remained staunchly behind their musical dream, the boys were able to pile into the family van and perform all over the Midwest.

Their parents' support went further than just chauffeuring them around, however. Although Tulsa has its share of local talent agents who book gigs for their clients, Hanson never went that route. They pretty much did it all on their own. Mom and Dad did the legwork, made the calls and got them bookings. No doubt Walker and Diana called on their own years of musical travel; they weren't complete novices at it. Ike, Taylor and Zac benefited from their parents' experience and willingness to help. Over the next few years, the Hanson Brothers got their musical feet wet, playing everywhere from the Oklahoma City State Fair to Branson, Missouri, to New Orleans, Louisiana.

And Tulsa, too. The boys still turned up regularly at local churches, at Tulsa's Big Splash Water Park and at Mayfest, where they became a yearly staple on the community stage. Naturally, as they grew, so did their music. Their harmonies got more intricate, their presentations just got better.

Everywhere they went, audiences responded enthusiastically. Ike, Taylor and Zac became more determined than ever to really make a professional go at the music biz. Yet no one had approached them about a recording contract.

To make that dream come true, the Hanson family realized they had to treat the boys' music as more of a business. The first step was actively soliciting fans to come and see them. They did that by compiling names and addresses of people who had already been in their audiences and, from that, making up a database mailing list. Then, whenever they scheduled a new gig, they'd send out mass mailings and newsletters, inviting all their fans to come see them. (Sometimes, when they played at schools, in lieu of payment the family would get a mailing list of all the students instead.)

The strategy was successful. Each new Hanson gig was attended by ever-larger audiences. It was those fans, in fact, who gave Ike, Taylor and Zac the idea for the next step in their climb up the musical ladder. For after each performance, invariably, a throng of kids would come up to the boys, asking for their autographs—*and* for info on where they could buy a Hanson album. Autographs was something Ike, Taylor and Zac could give; album info they could not.

Only they didn't see *why* not. Independent CDs and cassettes, on the most obscure labels, are recorded all the time—why couldn't the Hanson Brothers go into a local studio and do the same? They had more than enough material: amazing cover versions of classic R 'n' B songs, plus over fifty Hanson originals. If it worked out, they could not only give the fans what they wanted—a Hanson CD or cassette to take home after the show—but the brothers could also use the album as a polished, professional submission to major record labels.

It all made sense, except for one thing: On their

own, Ike, Taylor and Zac were nowhere near quali-
fied to produce an album. They needed professional
help.

Once again, they called on their parents' expertise
and willingness to investigate recording facilities in
Tulsa—and also on Mom and Dad's financial support. The Hanson Brothers needed to hire not just a
studio but musicians and producers as well. None of
whom come cheap.

It took some time, but after a few months of
inquiries and meetings with professional musicians
and producers, the Hanson Brothers were ready to
head into a local studio and record an album. The
decision was made to stick with doing covers of R 'n'
B songs and to not include any Hanson originals.
Again, since the boys had yet to learn instruments,
they sang along to backing tracks or with the studio
musicians they'd hired. Two producers were eventually employed to direct and mix the tracks.

The result was *Boomerang,* Hanson's 1995 debut
effort. While it got virtually no play on the radio, it
did get reviewed by at least one reporter on the local
beat. Jarrod Gollihare, a friend of the family, aspir-
ing musician and reporter for *Urban Tulsa* magazine, opined, not unkindly, that *Boomerang* was
"full of slick Boyz II Men meets Ace of Base style
pop."

Boomerang fulfilled at least part of its goal. For
Hanson did manage to sell copies of it wherever the
boys sang. If they played at a school or church where
they weren't allowed to sell merchandise, they simply passed out fliers so fans could place orders for

the record. In addition to the CD, the ever more enterprising clan designed and sold Hanson T-shirts.

The CDs and T-shirts were also available at local record stores. An employee at the Sound Warehouse in Tulsa explains, "The Hanson mom would come in with a pile of CDs and T-shirts for us to sell on consignment." In other words, the record store didn't pay any upfront money to stock *Boomerang*. They only made money if any copies were actually sold. Then all profits were split between the store and the Hansons; whatever stock didn't sell, the family took home. "They sold modestly," the sales-person remembers, "but really, the bulk of sales of the CDs were made at the live shows."

Isaac has since termed *Boomerang* "a pure R 'n' B record," and Taylor, for one, pinpoints *that* as the reason the album did not help fulfill the group's second goal: snaring the interest of a major record label. The boys sent it to every label they could find, but all they got back were rejections. "Record companies were afraid to sign us [on the basis of *Boomerang*]," Taylor told reporter Gollihare, "because we were white kids doing R 'n' B music, and it didn't exactly work."

Ike, Taylor and Zac determined to find another direction that would work.

DUES-PAYIN' DAYS

The Hansons decided to treat their first brush with rejection as a learning experience, pull back a bit and see what they could do differently. Around the same time, the boys were itching to expand musically anyway. The way to do that, they figured, was to learn to play instruments.

As Ike explains, "By 1995, we felt strongly that we wanted to be able to do it ourselves, to make our own music, not just sing it, but play it, instead of singing to a background tape all the time. Playing guitar gives you a whole different inspiration than the keyboard, and we needed those different inspirations."

Piano was the only instrument all three boys had taken lessons with and were fairly adept at. Therefore the transition to keyboards seemed natural Taylor, the most natural pianist of the trio, claimed that as his instrument. Alas, there were no keyboards lying around the Hanson home, and Taylor didn't have the money to buy a set.

No problem. "I ended up borrowing my first keyboards from a friend," Tay admits.

Isaac decided to follow in his dad's musical footsteps, picking guitar as his instrument. Only the Hansons, by that time, didn't own one of those anymore, either.

No problem. "I went to a pawn shop and got one," Isaac says.

Which left Zac. "He got stuck with the drums," Taylor says. "We just gravitated toward our choices first, and that's what was left for him. But he loves it."

A family friend confirms, "The bash and clatter of the drums was naturally attractive to Zac."

Zac has a different take on it all: "I couldn't play guitar or piano, so that's why I went with the drums. The secret is, no one else's arms were long enough. I was the only one who could play drums." Not that the Hansons had a set of those anywhere, either.

No problem. "A friend of ours had an old used Ludwig drum set in the attic," Zac tells. And in spite of the joking around, the youngest Hanson brother really did take a shine to them.

"In the beginning, we weren't very good at our instruments," Zac adds. "We're pretty much self-taught, and when we started playing, we just did simple stuff, bang, bang, bang."

Not being very good, however, didn't stop them

from taking their new instruments on the road, immediately. Ike explains, "We really wanted to play, so we just got out there and did it—we loved the instruments."

"Put it this way," Taylor says bluntly. "We got the drums and the instruments and a week later, we played live. But that doesn't mean we were good when we played live, it just means we got out there and did it."

Those first few times out with instruments didn't go without hitches. The boys hadn't reworked their staging quite enough. "We used to have a lot of dancing in our act," Taylor says, "so when we first added instruments, we'd switch off, we'd play, we'd dance."

Isaac admits that as a guitarist, he had a long way to go. "That first song we did with the guitar, I really didn't know the chords in that key, so I ended up playing this kind of riff thing."

Zac had his early problems too. "When we first started, these second-hand Ludwig drums that I had wouldn't stay still—they'd roll around the stage!"

The transition from straight *a cappella* vocal group to an actual band was awkward at best, and the boys knew they'd have to rethink certain aspects of their stage show. Eventually, as they improved on their instruments, they decided to ditch the dance steps altogether and give their all to just singing and playing.

And eventually, they were happier with the results. "Now," Isaac asserts, "singing and playing together has just become second nature."

SONGWRITING: "IT'S REALLY A HARD THING TO EXPLAIN"

Songwriting is something else that had become second nature to Ike, Taylor and Zac Hanson. They've often been quizzed about the process of composing songs and about what inspires them. To hear the Hansons tell it, it all comes naturally. And no one person—the eldest, for instance—has more say than anyone else. "Everybody contributes everything," Isaac declares. "It never happens that any one of us has more input than another. Generally, someone will start a song and everyone else will chime in."

Zac details, "It either works that way, or we'll all sit down together and write the whole song. It's just based on who has the best idea—"

"And we *will* debate over that," Isaac interrupts.

Some songwriters start with a melody and add lyrics later; for others, the process works the other way around. For Hanson, it all depends. "A lot of the time you write the music first," Isaac said in an interview last April. "But a lot of the time, music and lyrics are simultaneous—at least for me. For every person it's pretty much different, but in general, probably for us the music comes first. You generally play in a certain key and find some more abstract chords sometimes. It just comes to you."

Taylor concurs with Ike's assessment. "There's really no way to predict how you're going to write a song. It's an impossibility to know how it's going to happen, but I would say music first, because the music is what's inspiring you. But it's a hard question to answer definitively, because a lot of times you just never know. A lot of times we just jam and suddenly, the song will be there!"

Ike picks up the thread: "It's funny when people ask you how you write songs, because it's really a hard thing to explain. It happens in so many different ways, a lot of times the ones you find so intriguing, and are very dear to you, are the songs you can never explain why they came about. It just happens. Most of the time you start a song with just a feeling, just something you're thinking about, something that's going through your head. Or you just feel like writing something, so you sit down and play the guitar, or play the keyboard, and something begins to come out. Of course, sometimes nothing comes out!"

Taylor confirms, "There's no exact formula to writing a song. Every person has different thoughts, different methods."

Fourteen-year-old Taylor might have added that a lot of times you also "just never know" if you're going to end up writing about something you've actually experienced or that comes straight from your imagination.

"Our songs are inspired by everyday life," Taylor wrote in Hanson's record company bio. "Originally, we would write about [people we knew], our brothers and sisters. Just whatever we were thinking about."

Ike divulges, "All our songs are based on life, things that happen, y'know?"

"Inspiration comes from everyday life," Zac confirms. "Sometimes you can look out the window and something happens that'll inspire a song."

"Or," Taylor adds, "a lot of times we'll be inspired by just talking to friends, or hanging out with friends, or whatever. You get inspired and you write a song."

Naturally, thinking about girls is a great source of musical inspiration—but again, they haven't always experienced what they're writing about. "We were writing songs about girls and how sad it was when our girlfriends left us—back in the days when we thought girls had cooties!" Ike revealed with a chuckle during a TV interview. He quickly added that none of the Hanson boys feels that way any longer!

IKE, TAYLOR AND ZAC GO TO SCHOOL — SORT OF!

Girls have always cared about Hanson—even way back before most of the world knew there *was* a Hanson. From their earliest days playing local Tulsa gigs, the boys inspired fandemonium. An employee at their dad's company confides, "In Tulsa, Ike, Taylor and Zac had plenty of screaming little girls before they hit the big time. They were very, very popular. People would swamp them, wanting their autographs. So they have tasted fame, albeit on a smaller level."

A journalist confirms, "By 1995, they were known as this little white boy hip-hop trio that drove all the preteen girls mad. They'd built up a ravenous following of elementary-school kids."

There's a good reason for that. Ike, Taylor and Zac, who'd never gone to public school, frequently performed at several Tulsa elementary schools.

Pam Beckert, a secretary at Barnard Elementary School, has fond memories of the now instrumentally enhanced band who were still calling themselves the Hanson Brothers. "We'd have special assemblies for our Positive Action kids, those students involved in doing something good for their community, or raising drug awareness, or demonstrating what it really means to be honest. To honor them, we'd give out awards and offer entertainment during the ceremony."

Often the entertainment was musical—and on two memorable occasions, it was supplied by Ike, Taylor and Zac. Their upbeat songs and positive message fit the school's agenda perfectly.

"The first time during the '95–'96 school year," Ms. Beckert remembers, "they did a forty-five-minute set comprised of covers of old songs—no originals—and it went over really well, our kids were singing and humming as they filed out of the gym. So we invited the band back for a second performance, and this time they added some original Hanson songs to their repertoire. Again, our boys and girls really got into it—some even got up and were dancing in the aisles."

Ms. Beckert's niece Lani, a student there, remembers her reaction to the Hanson Brothers when they played at her school: "At first, I thought the drummer was a girl! And I thought Taylor was kinda cute. And I liked the way Isaac played and sang. But my favorite is Taylor."

Other performers who'd reached their level—playing Mayfest and already being on the state fair circuit—might view an appearance in an elementary-school gymnasium as a step backward, especially since the band rarely got paid for those kinds of gigs, and if they did, it was very nominal. But Hanson never looked at it that way. "It was always cool doing school assemblies," Ike has said, "because you're there to motivate kids to do what they want to do in life. Besides, the kids really responded well to us."

And Hanson responded well to the kids, too. During the shows, the boys would give away free Hanson T-shirts to any young audience member who raised his or her hand. "You could just come up onstage and get a T-shirt," Taylor recalls. "Once a girl raised her hand but was too embarrassed to come up—so Zac went out in the audience and personally escorted her up onstage to get her T-shirt!"

After each show, girls hung around the gym afterward, hoping to get a glimpse of them or, even better, talk to Ike, Taylor and Zac. The boys never just dashed away but spent as much time as necessary, talking to every person who wanted one-on-

31

one contact. Ms. Beckert remembers, "They interacted with the kids and were not full of themselves. They appreciated the audience as much as the audience appreciated them."

That appreciation went both ways when it came to *Boomerang,* their first CD. Many of the kids wanted to buy it at the end of the assembly, but it was against policy to actually sell albums at schools. So Ike, Taylor, Zac and their mom would simply pass out fliers and take orders for *Boomerang.* Then, a week or so later, the boys themselves came back to the school to deliver the albums.

Of course, school assemblies represented only a small segment of the types of gigs the Hansons had graduated to. On New Year's Eve 1995, they headlined Oklahoma City's Opening Night arts festival. An advertisement for the gig read, "Making their first appearance at Opening Night is Hanson, a vocal trio made up of three brothers from Tulsa. Hanson performs oldies from the '50s and '60s, as well as original songs."

The performances that were probably the most fun for Ike, Taylor and Zac had to be those on the stage of Tulsa's Big Splash Water Park, an all-water-rides amusement park featuring log flumes, speed slides and the biggest wave pool in Oklahoma. After they sang, Ike, Taylor and Zac got to put on their bathing suits and go on all the rides.

The boys had sung there in 1994, but the following year they had to reapply all over again, when new management took over. And it wasn't easy to rebook the gig, since the new person in charge, Becky

Thomas, didn't have time to listen to their CD and wasn't set on having them. So the boys' mom went to bat for them. A very persistent, very polite and very solid Diana Hanson won Ms. Thomas over with her enthusiasm and business savvy.

A deal was struck: Hanson would play, not for pay, but in exchange for season passes for the family *and* the right to set up a little booth where, at the end of the show, they could sell Hanson T-shirts and CDs. The boys also promised autographs and to pose for photos with fans. Even better, at their own expense, the Hanson family would send out a mailing, notifying their fans of the upcoming performance. It meant extra customers for Big Splash and a bigger crowd for Hanson. Win-win all around.

"The boys ended up playing twice that year," Ms. Thomas remembers, "and they were wonderful. They have such pure hearts—you can tell by the lyrics to their songs. One song was about not accusing someone else until you've walked in his shoes. Another that really stands out was about two figurines on the mantel, a one-armed soldier and a one-legged ballerina, and how they fell off the mantel and melted together, so they'd never have to be alone anymore. These were original songs, and so touching!"

What impressed Ms. Thomas most, however, was that the three boys would spend as much time as necessary at their booth after the show, until every last fan had gotten an autograph and photo. "They never rushed away to swim or go on the rides, even when it was broiling outside. They were never snobby, always courteous to everyone."

Most significant of all, when they had to leave to go on the road, their mom made sure they returned those season passes and didn't lend them out. "Their honesty and integrity is on par with their talent and pure hearts," Ms. Thomas says.

Clearly, Ike, Taylor and Zac's mom and dad have been megasupportive. The boys have always been grateful, as Ike expressed recently: "Our parents have really been good about just supporting us in general. They say, 'Guys, if you want to stop, we'll stop. If you want to keep going, and push harder, let's push harder.' They've just been there to back us up."

"Without them," Zac added ingenuously, "we couldn't drive to our shows!" The most spritelike Hanson added seriously, "Our parents didn't push us into this. This was our thing. But they helped us with it. They said, 'We're going to drive you where you want to go and get you what you need.'"

THE PARKING LOT GIG

As it turned out, one of the things Diana and Walker Hanson got for their sons was one of their most important gigs ever: the one at Tulsa's famous Blue Rose Café.

Along Tulsa's Peoria Drive arts and entertainment district, the Blue Rose Café is legendary. Described as "a hometown place for burgers, chili and fries," it boasts a happening nighttime scene. It's renowned as *the* place to hear live music, everything from classic rock to Cajun blues. Acts who play there get instant cool cachet and tend to be taken seriously by the entertainment press. Acts who play there, alas, are also always over twenty-one: The Blue Rose Café is very much a bar, and no one underage had ever been permitted to perform there.

Diana Hanson, however, was a friend of the owner's family, and by the summer of '95, her sons had gained a whole lot of musical cred all over town. The idea of Ike, Taylor and Zac appearing at the Blue Rose was broached. Eventually, the restaurant's owner came up with an idea for how the boys could play there without breaking the age-limit rules.

As Ike described it to MTV News, "Because it was a bar, we really couldn't play inside. But there's a large wooden deck outside the restaurant, where basically half the clientele sit and eat, especially during the summer." Just beyond that wooden deck was a parking lot area, and that's where it was decided Hanson could play.

Alex French, manager of the Blue Rose, explains, "We asked them to play around six P.M., which is several hours earlier than most of our acts go on. We'd never done anything like that before—never had an underage band play—plus we never had a band that played pop music like they did. They sounded like the Jackson 5, and everyone listening got into the fact that these kids were so young, and putting out such great music."

They sounded, actually, really good. In fact, that

first time, Hanson played three forty-five-minute sets. The first two featured completely different songs; the third was a mix, including Hanson originals and covers of such classics as "Do Wah Ditty," and "Poison Ivy." With each, the crowd at the restaurant, and those just strolling the sidewalk, got more and more enthusiastic. Taylor, who'd been wary of not being able to play inside the premises at first, soon realized that being outside was better. "People from all the surrounding restaurants could come over—and there are a lot of restaurants in that area!"

The Hansons also hedged their bets just a little, too. As soon as they got the booking, and realized they would be outdoors, they sent fliers to everyone on their mailing list, inviting one and all to come be part of the audience.

Many did. "There was a huge crowd of kids who'd seen them play at their schools and already owned their first independent CD, *Boomerang,*" remembers Tom Dittus, owner of the Blue Rose Café. "Ike, Taylor and Zac were young, and they weren't seasoned, but they knew how to handle and work a crowd. They were not nervous at all, very comfortable, confident performers. They just got up there and let it rip! They're really remarkable, so talented and such good kids. They've all got their heads on straight. They're very intelligent, extremely nice and well mannered—wholesome."

The band played the Blue Rose the following summer too, to thunderous response. That was the case everywhere Ike, Taylor and Zac played, and by 1996, they could count over 250 different gigs they'd played, some as local as Tulsa elementary schools, others as far away as Chicago, Kansas City, even Los Angeles.

"CAN WE PLAY FOR YOU?"

Austin, Texas, was another stop on Hanson's route. The state capital, Austin is well known for its burgeoning live music scene. Every March, the city plays host to the South by Southwest Music Conference, a major industry convention that brings together up-and-coming performers who want to get signed with agents, managers and record label representatives out to discover and sign up new talent. Which made it the perfect place for the Hanson Brothers. By 1995 they were eager to snag the attention of anyone who could help launch them into the music biz. According to South by Southwest organizers, Hanson wasn't officially booked to play there. However, many bands aren't. They just simply set up and play outside on the street, hoping to attract the attention of a passing music industry mogul. It works sometimes—it did for Hanson.

One such mogul was Christopher Sabac, a Los Angeles–based music attorney and manager, in Austin to scout new talent. He'd never heard of the Hanson Brothers, and he wasn't particularly looking for a group quite so young. In other words, he didn't seek them out. Nor did any of his professional peers.

No problem. Ike, Taylor and Zac simply found a

way to get Chris' attention: They stopped him on the street. As Taylor told *16* magazine, "We were doing our little song and dance, basically *a cappella*, with our boom box behind us. We just went up to him and said, 'Can we sing for you?' Then we put on a track of a song we had written and we just sang and danced for him. That's how we met him."

Chris Sabac described the meeting just slightly differently to journalist Paul Elliott: "I was having lunch in Austin, Texas, when the boys came up to me and asked if they could sing for me. Everyone else was ignoring them. They sang *a cappella* and I just said, 'Where are your parents? I need to talk to them fast!'"

Chris was bowled over—and won over—on the spot. His colleagues in the music industry, however, were not. The attorney later admitted, "Most record labels advised me to get away from this act as fast as possible. People said this act would ruin and humiliate me. It was very difficult."

But Chris would not be swayed by skeptics. He stuck to his first instinct, stuck by the band and signed on to manage them. Along with Ike, Taylor and Zac and their parents, he worked tirelessly to help them realize their dream. He knew it would be an uphill battle.

Back in Tulsa, according to a family friend, the Hanson family phone was ringing off the hook. There were many business calls, but even more were from squealing girls, wanting to talk to Ike, Taylor or

Zac. "They had to put an answering machine on that phone. They never pick it up without screening the calls first. They set up a second line for friends and family—that one's unlisted."

Clearly, the Hansons were getting ever more popular. And they knew the dream was getting closer to reality. They had professional management, were booked to perform constantly, sales of *Boomerang* were booming, and even more clearly, a fervent fan base was spreading.

And still, they did not have a record deal.

So once again, the family elected the do-it-yourself method. They went back into another local studio to record another independent CD. From the get-go, this one was going to be different than *Boomerang*.

As Isaac described it to *Urban Tulsa* magazine, "We went into a garage studio [actually, the Louis Drapp studio] and recorded our next album. We produced it ourselves and we played our instruments on it."

Taylor adds, "This time we did much more of a pop rock thing, because we were more of a pop rock group, now that we were playing instruments. There wasn't a lot of synth stuff on it. We completely wrote it."

During those sessions, it was Taylor who "cracked the whip" when Ike and Zac were goofing around. "He'd be the one to say, 'C'mon guys, let's get serious,' when Ike or Zac got goofy. Ike often broke into cartoon character voices, and Zac would just blurt out silly things at inappropriate moments," remembers Louis Drapp fondly. "We also had to record around Zac's stamina levels—we'd work for two hours or so, but then Zac would have to take a video game break."

They had a lot of material to choose from, as the boys had gotten ever more prolific. By 1996 they'd penned over a hundred songs. Of those, several were chosen for that second album. Three were tunes that would later end up on *Middle of Nowhere:* "Thinking of You," "With You in Your Dreams," and the one that CD is named for, "MMMBop."

That's right: The song Hanson became famous for in the spring of 1997 is not a new song—nor was it an easy one to compose. In fact, it wasn't even supposed to *be* a song! "We started [what would become "MMMBop"] in 1994," Isaac has revealed. "And it was a very long process, as far as the writing goes. It was first meant to be a background part for another song we were writing for *Boomerang.* [But] as time went on, it became too much of its own thing, took on a life of its own."

At the time, Ike, Taylor and Zac could not have known just what kind of a life "MMMBop" would take on—and lead them into!

DREAMS INTO REALITY

In May 1996, *MMMBop*, the indie album on the Hanson label, was ready to be released. As they'd done with *Boomerang*, the Hanson Brothers sold copies at their gigs—and, with help from their management this time, sent it out to record companies in hopes of landing a contract. This time, the results were very different. "There was lots of interest from record companies," Taylor acknowledges.

The record company showing the most interest was Mercury, a label that had actually rejected Hanson at least once before. Taylor thinks he knows the reason for the switch in attitude: "Because this time, we sounded like white kids doing what white kids actually do—rock 'n' roll."

At all major record labels, the people in charge of signing up new artists are referred to as "A & R guys": Artists and Repertoire directors (who, of course, aren't always guys). The vice president of Mercury's A & R department is Steve Greenberg. He is the person most responsible for championing Hanson at his label. As had been the case with manager Chris Sabac, Steve too had not gone looking to sign up a band so young. In an interview with *Billboard* magazine, he explained why. "A lot of A & R departments are worried about their own credibility if they sign a teen act, because in the past, a lot of teen acts, like New Kids on the Block, were wholly manufactured."

For that reason, he was very skeptical of Hanson. In an interview with the *New York Times,* Steve described his reaction upon hearing the independently produced *MMMBop* album: "I got this tape and I loved it—but I was convinced it was fake. I thought maybe they had been manufactured. I was sure there was some adult pulling the strings, or the vocals were manipulated, and they weren't really playing their instruments. I wasn't going to [pursue it further]."

Still, there was something magical about that title song that made Steve overcome his initial skepticism. At least he was intrigued enough to shlep from his New York City office all the way out to the hamlet of Coffeyville, Kansas, a small town just over the Oklahoma border and not very far from Tulsa. That's where Hanson was performing at the county fair. As soon as Steve saw Ike, Taylor and Zac sing and play their instruments, he knew his trip had been well worthwhile. Nothing was manipulated; no one was pulling the boys' strings. "They played great, they sang great—they completely re-created the music on the tape live. They sang as well as they sang on the record, and played as well as they played on the record—and I was surprised on both counts," Steve admits. "And they did it all themselves, there wasn't an adult in sight, except their dad, who was loading up the equipment, and their mom, who was selling T-shirts."

That very day in June, 1996, Steve Greenberg offered Hanson a recording contract on the Mercury label. It took less than an "MMMBop" moment for the boys to accept the offer. Little did they know that from that moment on, their lives would zoom into fast forward! Ike, Taylor and Zac barely had time to savor their victory—the beginning of their dream coming true.

For as soon as they signed on the dotted line with Mercury, the head-spinning big-league wheels went into motion. It was decided that Hanson would be swept off to Los Angeles immediately, to record an all-new album for the label. While the album would retain the flavor of Hanson's independent efforts, it would need to incorporate other ideas as well.

For as blown away as Steve had been by "MMMBop," he knew that to make it, and to be respected in the world of rock 'n' roll, Hanson would benefit from a professional helping hand. Or several. "I felt they needed a lot of mentoring," Steve admitted to *Dot Music* magazine. "They needed to be around people who could really help them make the right kind of record."

To *Billboard,* he added, "Many people who have

dealt with kids on records have taken a fairly conde-
scending approach and made very young-sounding
records, without a great deal of musical credibility.
The music the Hansons had written demanded
greater care than that."

It's easy to see how Ike, Taylor and Zac might have
felt overwhelmed by the idea of experts being recruited to work with them. Another band, in fact,
might have felt intimidated—possibly even under-
mined. But to their credit, the Hanson brothers did
not protest the label's hands-on method but rolled
with it—even though the idea of incorporating
established master song-crafters into their personal
creative process had to be unsettling.

"It was weird at first," Ike admitted to journalist
Jarrod Gollihare. "Just learning to work with other
people, to exchange ideas—"

"And not to irritate each other," Taylor broke in,
then added, "We weren't so much nervous, as [we]
just felt strange 'cause we didn't know what it was
going to be like. We've always done the writing and
arranging by ourselves."

Still, they were more than open to finding out. On
the whole, the boys felt that they'd signed on with a
team that was fully behind them. And they appreciated it. "We were getting a lot of enthusiasm from
the label," Ike told a reporter. "And that's really
good, because you can't go anywhere unless the label
is behind you."

Were they ever! Steve and his staff went about
gathering the hottest and the hippest music professionals—songwriters, arrangers and producers—

they could find: people who'd add that dash of cachet to the Hanson sound and really take it through the roof. "We were looking for producers who were incredibly creative and attuned to what was going on," Steve said.

They found 'em. The list of luminaries lined up by Mercury Records to collaborate on the Hanson album is amazing!

The first person Steve thought of was a writer and producer named Steve Lironi, who'd worked with British groups Space and Black Grape. "The Black Grape record *It's Great When You're Straight . . . Yeah!* is one of the best-arranged records I'd heard in a long time, so I suggested Steve Lironi. [Hanson] needed help with arrangements—that was the most important thing."

Steve Lironi did more than lend an arranging hand to Hanson. He's credited with co-producing their album and co-writing the songs "Speechless," and "Look at You."

Other songwriting stars recruited for the Hanson album included the legendary team of Barry Mann and Cynthia Weil. Known for scores of hits, including the Righteous Brothers classic "You've Lost That Lovin' Feelin'," the pair worked with Ike, Taylor and Zac on the romantic ballad "I Will Come to You."

Desmond Child, revered in rock circles as a premier song doctor, has Bon Jovi and Aerosmith on his list of credits. He worked with the young band on the haunting ballad "Weird."

Ellen Shipley is responsible for penning "Heaven

Is a Place on Earth" for Belinda Carlisle. Her work appears on the Hanson track "Yearbook."

The songwriter who worked with the young band first, and most extensively, however, is Mark Hudson. Over the past decade, he has become one of L.A.'s most in-demand tunesmiths, and he has written tracks for such rockers as Bon Jovi and Aerosmith, including the latter's most famous song, "Livin' on the Edge."

Mark had not heard of the Tulsa trio before getting the call from Steve Greenberg, but an instant sense of déjà vu hit him as soon as the young band came knocking at his studio door. For Mark didn't start out in the music biz as a songwriter: Once upon a time, he too was part of a very young singing group. His partners were his brothers, Bill and Brett. Back in the late 1970s, they were known as the Hudson Brothers. They had hit records, a CBS-TV variety show, and were bona fide teen idols covered regularly by such publications as *16* magazine.

"It was uncanny," Mark remembers. "The idea of going from the Hudson Brothers to the Hanson Brothers was kind of cool. It all sounded so parallel. I'd been there, done that, I knew all about working with the family dynamic. And there really *is* a family dynamic, whether it's the Osmonds, the Jacksons, the Bee Gees, the Hudsons or the Hansons. There is something special musically about being a family."

Mark clearly recalls the day the entire Hanson family came to his studio for the first time. "They were adorable. I saw a younger, blonder version of my brothers and myself. They brought their guitar and their ideas, and we got to work. They're really, really talented, and so eager to learn. I was really impressed with them."

Ike, Taylor and Zac were impressed with Mark too. They were aware of the Hudson Brothers, but not of Mark's subsequent songwriting success. They were awed by the photos of the artists Mark has worked with that line his studio walls, including the Beatles (John Lennon was actually a personal friend of the Hudson Brothers way back when) and Aerosmith's Steven Tyler. Imagine how they felt when, out of the blue, Steven Tyler happened to call the studio during one of their sessions. They were blown away!

Because of Mark's background, he, perhaps more than anyone on the Hanson's new team, approached the album as a family project. "Even though Taylor is the lead singer, I wanted to contribute a song for each brother," he says. The concept got a unanimous thumbs-up from Hanson. And so, from their work with Mark, the Hansons emerged with three songs for their album. The rocker "Where's the Love?" is Taylor's lead, but Ike takes over on "A Minute Without You." The lovely, lilting "Lucy" is Zac's first stab at lead honors.

Working with Mark Hudson was a comfortable, mega-positive experience for the band, but it wasn't the only high point in the making of what would become *Middle of Nowhere*.

Ike, Taylor and Zac were completely awed by the duo brought in to do overall production on the album, for producers don't come any hipper, or with more musical credibility, than the Dust Brothers. Not really brothers, John King and Michael Simpson are currently the high priests of all that's ultra-hip, cool and cutting edge in rock 'n' roll production. They're the pair behind *Odelay,* the Grammy-winning album by the ultra-hip, cool and cutting edge artist Beck.

Any band the Dust Brothers sign up to work with garners insty-cred within the music industry. So why would the DBs put their stamp of approval on a band so untested and so young as Hanson? Mike Simpson offers a simple reason: "They write their own songs and play their own instruments. These kids are definitely the real deal."

Now, Ike, Tay and Zac are ultra-blasé about their brush with über-hipness. "The Dust Brothers, they have a very clean house," Zac quipped on MTV's *Week in Rock* show. Taylor added, "They're not really dusty. I actually was looking for the dust."

Cute. But when they were first introduced, Hanson was as awed as they should have been. And as far as Ike, Taylor and Zac were concerned, the Dust Brothers very much lived up to their hyperbolic rep. "They were really cool to work with," Isaac told *Urban Tulsa* magazine. "The whole vibe of the studio was very laid back. We'd come there about noon and sit down and talk a little while, and when we felt like starting, we would. And they have a great record collection, obviously, 'cause they use a lot of different sampled things. So they'd play us different records—everything from the Pointer Sisters to

Three Dog Night to all the Beatles songs. It was really cool."

Though the famed production pair didn't contribute specific songs to the album, their influence is felt throughout. As Isaac puts it, "They added some interesting elements that we might not have thought of. 'MMMBop' is a good example. They added a 'ruh-uh-ruh-uh-ruh-uh' scratch thing. But that's really all the scratching that's on the album."

Taylor adds, "I think what the Dust Brothers and Steve Lironi kinda brought back to our sound was a little of the R 'n' B—with the loops and scratches and sampled sounds—and combined it with pop-rock."

For the smallest singing Hanson brother, the best part of working with the Dust Brothers was totally nontechnical: Zac liked getting to mess around outdoors in their swimming pool. "We jumped in with our clothes on!" he exclaims.

The entire Hanson family spent five months in Los Angeles while Ike, Taylor and Zac recorded *Middle of Nowhere.* For the most part, the whole experience—working with so many different people, living in a completely different environment—was challenging but positive. "We learned a lot," Ike says. "And we worked a lot."

"Recording an album is tedious," Zac adds, "but it's fun. We love to sing, but there's a lot of work involved in making a CD happen."

Not to mention a dab of trauma too—like when Taylor's voice suddenly changed halfway through the making of the album. "If you listen closely, you'll hear my voice is about four notes lower at the end of the album than it was at the beginning!"

Luckily, the Dust Brothers, Steve Lironi and Mark Hudson, who handled much of the vocal direction, had the skill to overcome that problem. No one but Taylor, who's the most sensitive to it, can really tell.

Middle of Nowhere turned out to be a truly collaborative effort. While the boys did get the chance to play their instruments on each track, their work was buttressed by a total of fifteen studio musicians to help fill out their sound. Which Hanson doesn't see as a negative comment on their musical shortcomings but, rather, as an extra added bonus for the listener. As Zac expresses it, "[All those other musicians playing is] another cool thing in there."

One of many cool things, in fact. Issac's take after hearing the album in its entirety was this: "There's quite a bit of variety to the songs. Some make you want to dance, they're really up and make you feel good. And other ones are really intense, they're like, 'Wow, what's this about?' And some are just mellow. We wrote every one and every one has a different meaning for us."

The man who'd signed them up, Steve Greenberg, was equally juiced about the result. His idea to surround Hanson with those particular co-writers and producers had paid off. "A lot of the excitement about the album comes from the fact that [Hanson's] classic style songs are produced in a totally contemporary fashion," he told *Billboard*.

While Ike, Taylor and Zac were pumped about

Middle of Nowhere, they weren't naive. They knew that skepticism and criticism were just around the corner. They'd heard it for the last five years on a smaller scale; now that they were poised to enter the big time, they assumed the carping would just get louder. As Taylor told *Billboard* right before *Middle of Nowhere*'s release, "People are going to say, 'Oh, they're young kids, they don't play, they don't write, they were put together, something's got to be screwy about them.' But you have to listen to the album— the music speaks for itself."

That the music on *Middle of Nowhere* is pure power pop, and lacks the alterna-angst that has fueled the music biz for so many years, was also cause for concern. Hanson is prepared to be attacked for their style. "I'm sure people will say that we're a novelty act, but we're not and we don't plan to be. It's just their perception of it. Even though being a kid is kind of a carefree sort of thing for the most part, there are definitely a lot of things that stick in kids' minds," Ike says.

Adds Zac bluntly, "We don't have as many problems as grown-ups!"

They certainly had no problem being in Los Angeles for the five months it took to record the album. Although most of their time was spent inside studios, the brothers did enjoy being in showbiz land. They lived in a rented home high atop the Hollywood Hills. "You could actually see the famous 'Hollywood' sign from the deck on the back of the house," Ike told a reporter. "And on the other side, you could look down and see Mann's Chinese Theater. There's so much to see in Los Angeles, it's very cool."

Which isn't to say the brothers didn't get homesick. "By the time we finished the album, we were definitely ready to come home to Tulsa," Taylor confesses. But an affinity for Los Angeles has stayed with them. They've been back to the city several times in the last year, so often that it almost feels like "a home away from home," as Taylor puts it.

Little did they know that soon the band would feel comfortable in many cities, not only in the U.S.A., but around the world. They may have sprung from the Middle of Nowhere, but thanks to the album with that title, they would soon be in the spotlight, front and center, in the Middle of Everywhere!

IKE: THE SLY ONE

As a group, the Hanson brothers are bright, charming, chatty and witty—as long as the conversation centers around their music, that is. They gladly recap their musical history, their influences, the slow but steady climb to the top; and of course, they never forget to say how grateful they are to everyone who's helped them. In fact, the boys will tell you anything you want to know—unless the questions delve too deeply into their personal lives, that is!

The true scoop on Hanson is this: None of the three is very comfortable talking about himself. It's not that anyone's hiding a deep dark secret, just that all are truly modest. Still, hang with Hanson long enough, and a picture of each boy starts to emerge. Ike, the sly one, might purposely (albeit politely) duck a particular question; Taylor might really be

53

too shy to answer; Zac, the resident ham on wry, is too busy being a clown!

Oldest brother Isaac, who prefers being called Ike, has been portrayed as "the serious one," but that's not really fair. A study in contrasts is closer to it. Ike's a complex mix of the serious and the silly, the calm and crazy, the introspective and the outspoken all at the same time. Above all, and without being a snob, he has a quiet confidence.

His passion is music, and not just his own. Ike's a true musical historian, whose interest in vintage tunes goes way deeper than those '50s and '60s Time/Life compilations he's talked so much about. Ike is also into more obscure, yet influential genres and can discourse intelligently about tunes from the early rap label Sugarhill or pioneering R 'n' B tracks from the now obsolete Stax label.

Yet even when it comes to music, Ike's got a silly streak a mile deep. When a newspaper reporter positively gushed over Hanson's *Middle of Nowhere* album, Isaac cracked, "Too bad you can't marry it."

Yes, he was being a bit of a smart aleck, but that doesn't mean Ike isn't sincerely grateful for Hanson's success. "It's completely fulfilling our expectations if not exceeding them," he humbly told a reporter from the *New York Times*. "You can't ever expect to have a Top 10 single, you can only hope to maybe reach the Top 40. And to be played on MTV as much as we've gotten played is incredible. We didn't think people would think we're cool enough."

Not that Ike ever felt that way. He's the realist of

the bunch; an Ike-eye view of the world takes in everything. While he acknowledges other people's perceptions of himself and his brothers, he doesn't necessarily share them. He'd never bend to trends, or change anything about himself just to be cool. Especially not his music. Ike's aware that alternative music has ruled the scene over the last few years, when Hanson was trying to get a break. But it never once occurred to him to write an angry, angst-filled tune just to be in step with the times. "We were always doing [the kind of music] we love to do," Ike told *MTV News*. "We weren't worrying about what other bands were doing. We do what we do. And they do what they do. That's the way of the world. Besides, there's enough hard stuff in life, plenty of stuff to get down about. For us, music is a way to get away from things."

Isaac is proud of Hanson music, but he's not down with comparisons to other groups, whether favorable (the Beatles, once) or unfavorable (NKOTB, Menudo, more than once). "Don't go there," he once beseeched a journalist. "You never want to compare yourself to anyone else."

Something else Ike doesn't like is being pigeonholed—music-wise or image-wise. Like his brothers, Ike's sensitive to being tagged and dismissed as just another teen idol, incapable of making legitimately good music. "We know some people will automatically be biased toward our age, but we take our music very seriously, and hopefully, we'll have a very broad audience," he's declared.

While he and his brothers are willing to be interviewed by teen magazines, they have balked at being photographed. At one such encounter, Ike agreed with Hanson handlers in protesting the absence of hair and makeup professionals. He may be a new-comer, but he's clear about standing up for himself. Isaac simply feels that Hanson deserves to be presented in the best possible light, and if that is not possible, they should just politely decline a shoot altogether. Which they did. (Later they did pose for the magazines, but with their own photographer, and on their terms.)

Clearly, Ike has a strong sense of himself—but that doesn't translate into being full of himself. He does not have an inflated ego. He may not cringe when he sees himself on TV or on video, but he doesn't beam with pride either. Sometimes he admits to being just plain mystified. "I'll listen to a tape of ours and go, 'That's me? No way!' But once you get used to hearing yourself, you get to enjoy making music and hearing it."

Musically, Ike is the driving force behind Hanson. But he's far from a bully. He completely respects the opinions of the other members of the group—even if they happen to be his little brothers. And although he has a strong rock 'n' roll lead singer's voice, he's not at all jealous that Taylor takes front-and-center vocals on most songs. That was a decision Hanson made together.

Isaac doesn't even get to be the main spokesperson for Hanson. In interview situations, he's vocal and articulate, but he inevitably gets interrupted by Taylor or Zac.

Ike doesn't really mind. The brothers have always had a smooth relationship, even when they were a lot younger. When asked what they squabble about, all Ike can come up with is this: "Taylor and I used to practice karate on each other, but we can't anymore, 'cause we'd really hurt each other. Now we may tease each other from time to time, but that's about it." Ike and Taylor truly are best friends; they get each other's jokes and often choose to hang out together even when they're not working.

Within the family, Ike takes his older brother role seriously. "He really looks out for the little ones," observes Mark Hudson, the songwriter who worked closely with them on *Middle of Nowhere*. A 1994 article in *Tulsa World* tagged Ike "the responsible one," observing that he "acts as the group's organizer and producer." Taylor was quoted as saying, "He makes sure we've got all the pitch pipes with us."

The calmest of the bunch, Ike claims that little if anything gets on his nerves—except maybe the sound of fingernails on a chalkboard. "That gives me goosebumps," he allows.

For all his earnest self-confidence, Ike does have a wild and crazy side. "I'm definitely very goofy," he told *MTV News,* "goofy-stupid." He's the Hanson known for his impressions of famous folks, both fictional and real; he cracks up his family and friends with his Beavis and Butthead impersonation.

Although he's been mega-busy with the worldwide launch of Hanson, Ike hasn't neglected his schoolwork. He just completed his sophomore year of high school, and in September he'll start his junior year.

Mom's still his main teacher, but Ike now has a math tutor as well.

A gifted writer, Ike's been working on a science-fiction novel for the past two years. He hopes to get it finished soon.

On those rare occasions when Ike's not writing or working on his music or his schoolwork, he's often outside rollerblading or playing street hockey. "We all love to play all sports," he asserts.

DRESSING TO IMPRESS? NOT!

When it comes to fashion, none of the Hanson hunks are slaves to the latest styles. Ike, especially, is indifferent to logos, designers, what's in or what's five minutes ago. And don't think he hasn't been dissed for it. One magazine even termed Hanson fashion as "dweeby '70s thrift store clothes." But just as he wouldn't change his music to be in tune with the times, Ike would never change his look just to fit someone else's definition of what's in style.

His tastes run to the simple and comfortable. Ike's likes include patterned button-down long-sleeve shirts, often worn open over a solid-color T-shirt. He favors khakis or slouchy and baggy sweat pants over jeans, and high-top sneakers or Timberlands over Docs or chic running shoes. His colors of choice tend to be dark and earthy—lots of browns, grays, forest greens and burgundys.

The oldest Hanson wears little jewelry; the only two constants are a silver ring on the middle finger of his left hand and a wristwatch on his right. His other everyday accessory is dental: Ike smiles proudly, displaying his braces. If people think that looks dorky, that doesn't bother self-assured Ike. Vain, he's not!

WHAT'S YOUR SIGN?

Like lots of teenagers, the Hanson brothers are aware of their astrological signs. They don't check their horoscopes daily nor make decisions based on the stars, but it is uncanny how well their personalities fit their astrological profiles. What can fans glean from the Hanson sun-sign scene? Lots, in fact.

Isaac celebrates his birthday on November 17, which makes him a Scorpio. As such, Ike is a born leader, cool, composed and charismatic. That last trait is especially evident when he's up onstage, guitar in hand, performing.

Self-assured and self-aware, Isaac seems to know exactly what he is and what he isn't. When a Scorpio is convinced he's right, there's little anyone can say or do to change his mind. He's rarely rattled by insults or, conversely, swayed by flattery. Isaac's honest and has great integrity. He respects those qualities in others.

Ike believes in himself and his family, and he has strong faith in the Hanson ability to overcome obstacles. In fact, adversity brings out the best in him. It's little wonder that Ike never wanted to quit trying to make it in the music biz, even though the Hanson brothers met with rejection so often. Perseverance comes naturally to Scorpios. Competition just makes them work harder.

Ike makes up his mind quickly; he's hardly ever plagued by indecision, whether about a new lyric, what to wear, or whether he wants someone for a friend. Intensely loyal, smart and generous, there's nothing Ike wouldn't do for a friend or family member. As the big brother in the family, Ike is mega-responsible and gently protective of all his younger siblings.

Fans sometimes find him hard to figure out, since his expression often gives nothing away. But a Scorpio's smile is always genuine, as is that haunting sweetness people who know him well can always detect.

TAYLOR: THE SHY ONE

The middle Hanson brother has been described in print as everything from "a pubescent Kurt Cobain" to "a dreamboat so fine featured most people mistake him for a girl." Of course, the person who wrote that last line was not a girl, because no female Hanson fan has ever made that mistake. Indeed, to the gazillions of girls who go ga-ga for Taylor, he's all-boy, all-hottie, majorly swoon-worthy.

It's not just that fourteen-year-old Taylor's the lead singer—traditionally, girls do go for the guy up front—or that Tay's the one with the big blue eyes, that sexy curling lip, or even because of that sweet gap-toothed mile-wide smile. More likely, it's Tay's personality shining through that inspires all those "I Love Taylor" signs, all that screaming and all that dreaming of meeting him one day. Not to mention several Internet sites devoted exclusively to him, designed and maintained by Tay's inventive techno-babe fans.

Taylor is the most enigmatic Hanson, the one who probably *is* harboring a few secrets no one knows. "I'm the quietest one, obviously," is what he told *MTV News*. Taylor really is the shy one, the serious one, the one who blushes most easily, and easily the most modest of the trio.

How modest? Put it this way: All evidence to the contrary—like eleven songs out of thirteen on the album—Taylor tries to dodge being tagged as the lead singer, insisting, "Part of what Hanson is, is that there's not just one guy who sings. Having three voices is what makes us Hanson."

When asked how it feels to be this successful this young, Taylor may goof around with Ike: "Actually, we thought we'd be younger—we were just saying, 'Man, we're too old now!'" But he'll quickly revert to his true feelings and gently say, "You can never expect to be this successful; you can only work for it, and hope for it. But to hear Casey Kasem announce that you're Number One in his countdown, and to look in *Billboard* and see your name, *that* is really cool."

Ironically, the heartthrob Hanson in the spotlight is the one least drawn to it. It's not that Taylor doesn't appreciate his fans, but he'd really rather not be singled out as the most popular of the boys. He's always seen himself as a third of a trio, no more nor less deserving than Ike or Zac. It's weird to be perceived otherwise by thousands of fans.

How shy is Taylor? Depends on the situation. If

he's being interviewed—clearly something he's not at ease with—watch his body language: Taylor's the one with his arms crossed in front of him. And unlike Ike, Taylor still admits to not being comfortable when hearing Hanson on the radio. "It's always weird to hear yourself," he confides.

Of course, put him in front of a keyboard, synthesizer, set of congas and an audience, and watch the bashfulness morph to confidence. Like all pure performers, Taylor's most at home up onstage doing what he loves to do, instead of being offstage, having to talk about it.

Being shy doesn't prevent him from standing up for himself or expressing his beliefs. As many a journalist will attest, when you do get him talking, Taylor's the Hanson who can be counted on to give the straightest, most thoughtful answers. When quizzed about Hanson's anti-alterna vibe, Taylor doesn't react defensively, merely honestly. "Music's always changing, just like styles are always changing," he told *MTV News*. "I think things are going away from the alternative thing. Just because the music we make is more up, and more fun, I guess in a way [Hanson probably is] where music is headed."

Like Ike, he'd rather not be compared with other musicians, but he does have a sense of humor about it. When a Beatles comparison was made, Taylor quipped, "The Beatles! I mean, they were the Beatles! We're ladybug size."

Like his brothers and sisters, Taylor is homeschooled by Mom and Dad. In September he'll be in ninth grade—the beginning of his high-school years.

So far, Taylor's favorite subjects have been literature and art.

All three Hanson brothers are talented artists, but Taylor's renderings really stand out. He draws in pen and pencil, chalk, with markers or crayons; on paper, napkins, or an easel, whatever's handy. His portraits are amazingly accurate, as songwriter Mark Hudson attests: "Taylor drew a picture of me wearing a beret, with a 'bubble' coming out of my mouth that made it look like I was saying 'Groovy.' Taylor just thought it was funny that I say 'groovy' so much."

The portrait really captures Mark as Taylor sees him. Generous Tay gave Mark the drawing as a gift.

In fact, although Taylor is shy, once you get to know him, he's incredibly soft-hearted, generous and very much a talker. A good friend offers, "Taylor can sometimes be the quiet one, but sometimes he'll talk your ear off as well." He loves pizza, is always up for a game of soccer or one-on-one basketball, and he listens to all kinds of music, everything from country to rap—yes, even alternative.

TAYLOR-ING HIS LOOK

Like his older brother, Tay's not swayed by what the fashion mags say is in. Function above fashion is his motto. "We really just wear what we want to wear, what's comfortable," Taylor once declared. For him, that means lots of Hang Ten T-shirts, once in a while under a long-sleeved, open-buttoned denim or solid red shirt, but most often without other layers.

While Ike usually sticks to earth tones, Tay's Ts come in all colors, and most are V-necks. He wears a lot of blue (to offset his eyes?), some black, a bit of green, red or gray. At one gig, he showed up in a killer teal leather jacket; at another, a black denim jacket. For a photo shoot once, he wore an electric-blue long-sleeved shirt with white stripes.

Taylor's the Hanson most likely to be in jeans, either blue or black, or blue baggies like the ones he wore on *The Jenny McCarthy Show.* He rarely wears sneakers or running shoes but opts for hiking boots similar to Timberlands or Doc Martens.

While he eschews rings or earrings, Taylor is the most accessorized Hanson: Aside from an ever-present wristwatch, he wears a profusion of pendants around his neck, often four or five at a time. All are short enough to count as chokers. A few are beads threaded on ropy leather straps, one's a silver coin, another resembles an ankh (an Egyptian good luck symbol); sometimes he'll wear religious symbols, sometimes not.

And in a nod to his newfound celeb status, he does wear a beeper. Taylor tries to keep it somewhat hidden, however, clipped to the back of his waist, so as not to be showy about it. That's not what he's about.

WHAT THE STARS SAY

Born on March 14, Taylor seems to be a totally typical Pisces. Creative and artistic, spiritual and imaginative, the family dreamboat is also the family dreamer. But it's probably not a pot of gold at the end of Tay's reverie rainbow; more likely visions of new music dance in his head, or new canvases to paint on. For Pisces are the least materialistic people on the planet; flash and cash don't move them, nor does the promise of fame and fortune. The Pisces is the pure artist in the family who just wants to create.

Just as his brother Ike is a born leader, Taylor's a born performer. Being able to project the emotions in a song, not just sing the lyrics, comes naturally—whether he's experienced them or not. Pisces are sensitive and sympathetic to the problems of others and hardly ever judgmental.

As fits his Piscean nature, Tay is easygoing and good-natured, and he's astoundingly indifferent to personal insults. Tell him he's oft mistaken for a girl and he'll just shrug it off. "That happens a lot. I don't mind. It's pretty funny." Tell him of the skeptics out there who don't believe Hanson really composes their own music, he reacts, as he did in a VH-1 interview, with understanding. "You're going to get that. . . . You see three kids making music where the oldest is hardly old enough to drive . . . it's natural to be suspicious. I would be too, but this is what we do, this is who we are."

Criticize his music, however, and he becomes sensitive. It's his passion, after all. It isn't unusual for Pisces to be naturally shy, and to shy away from competition—which is one reason he and his more ambitious, competitive brother Ike work so well together: Their strengths complement each other.

A Biography

It takes a lot to anger a Pisces, although Taylor can have occasional temper tantrums. However, he's quick to forgive, and he rarely holds a grudge. Just like the Hanson music he makes, Tay prefers to see things sunny side up; his glass is always half full.

ZAC: THE HAM ON WRY ONE

Incoming: a Zac attack! Everyone better duck! By far the most outrageous, most over-the-top and too adorable for words Hanson, blond, brown-eyed, pillow-lipped Zachary Walker just can't help himself. Hyper-wired and wacky, he's the born attention-getter of the family. He's the one who'll break into impromptu karate kicks and speak in triple exclamation points!!! Really!!! The band Hanson has been called "spontaneously rambunctious": everyone agrees that Zac's the Hanson most likely to spontaneously combust. Figuratively speaking, that is.

Speaking of which, journalists describing Zac pull out all the stops from their figurative bag of metaphors and similes. To wit, Zac's been tagged "the here-comes-trouble kid," "the official comic relief," "the resident hyper-drive," "the ham," "the Jim

Carrey-in-training," "the funny one," "the una-bashed crazy one," "easily the clown of the band, not afraid to be boisterous and stupid," and once, even though it wasn't printed, "the Ritalin kid."

Yakkety Zac, never at a loss for words, takes on all comers.

Is he the joker of the band? You make the call.

"Our parents forced us into this!" Zac jubilantly blurted out during one interview, and "No, we *don't* get along," during another, as he playfully punched Taylor and then jumped on Ike's back, his arms dangling around his brother's neck, gorilla-style. "I just joined the band because two-part harmony didn't really sound too right, they needed a third person." When a writer mentioned a trip he'd be taking, Zac advised him, "Don't jump off the plane!"

Is he a ham? "No, I'm a chicken," Zac zaps back.

Is he the here-comes-trouble kid? Watch him incite an already feverish crowd by pretending to jump into a mosh pit of fans, or over a railing, or simply urging them to scream . . . louder!!! All three of which he did at Hanson's appearance at Universal Citywalk in May.

Is he hyper? According to insiders, Zac never walks when he can run, nor is he apt to be silent when he can talk. Indeed, Zac does not like to be left out of a conversation. During an *MTV News* inter-view, which had gone on, oh, about two minutes with questions directed at Ike and Tay, Zac piped up, "You know, *I'm* not talking here!" A few min-utes later, he pretended to fall asleep altogether! In another interview, he responded to all questions with nonsensical noises, like "zzbbdu," and "hunn-huh," and the ever-popular "kapow!" Zac makes sure everyone knows he's there.

Once, in a rare moment of quasi-introspection, Zac offered up a reason for his hyper-kinetic behavior: "I think it's probably that I'm so shy that I just act wacky to make up for it."

Or not. Most people who know him think *that's* the joke: Zac just really is a major, always-in-motion extrovert. He doesn't even take himself seriously. To a reporter he joshed, "The first time I saw our video on MTV, I said, 'Look at that cute girl. No, wait! It's me!'"

So is Zac ever serious, about anything? If it took longer than a split second to guess "His music," you don't know Hanson as well as you might. For Zac's all business when that subject comes up. He sounds just like a savvy business pro when he asserts, "Our music isn't just for teens. We've gotten good response from old guys too—college guys."

Nor, in spite of his own tender years, is he keen on Hanson being stuck with a strictly teenybop image. During a potential photo shoot at the offices of a teen magazine, it was Zac who objected most vociferously to posing in front of what he perceived as a "juvenile" backdrop. It was pink.

He was extremely wary when asked what his favorite color was. "Blue," he answered in a measured tone. "Why are you asking me that?"

But speaking strictly of his music, *seriously,* Zac may well be the most gifted musician in the family.

He really is a prodigiously talented drummer—not just for his age but for any age. Ike and Tay are not just indulging their younger brother in the creative process. Still a year away from even being a teenager, Zac is a full participant in writing Hanson lyrics; composing the music, he's instinctively able to "hear" what's wrong in a song-in-progress.

And for all his joking around, at heart, Zachary is really modest. "I'm not that great a drummer," he once said. "But everybody says I can play, so I'll take their word for it." Speaking for his brothers, Zac added, "We don't necessarily think we're the big shots."

In many ways, Zac's the most open Hanson, the easiest to get to know. He's not sly, he's certainly not shy; he's just out there. What you see—and hear—is, refreshingly, what you get. "Goofy-funny," he calls himself.

A home-schooled sixth-grader, Zac's best subject is math and, of course, art. Like Taylor, he's an extremely accomplished cartoonist; unlike Tay, Zac doesn't limit himself to ordinary mediums or canvases. In fact, anything at hand will do. One writer witnessed Zac's "masterwork of neo-modernist portraiture . . . rendered in extra fancy ketchup and packaged honey, done on a used paper plate."

Imaginative Zac does impersonations: TV commercials and southern drawls are his specialties. He loves video games like Laserquest, and he's neither too old nor too embarrassed to still enjoy playing with action figures. His Power Rangers go everywhere with him, including the recording studio.

Mark Hudson chuckles, remembering Zac plopping down on the floor of his studio, making up imaginary battles with his Power Rangers as everyone got ready to discuss the next song.

DRESSING UP

While none of the Hanson hotties could be called a style-conscious clothes horse, the one who comes closest is Zac. He's the brother with another mindset: He'll do bright colors, zany fabrics, the no-one-but-Zac-could-wear-that-and-get-away-with-it stuff.

Under a black V-neck sweater, he's worn a velour top—in bright orange. In Los Angeles for a press conference, Zac turned up in taxi-cab yellow satiny parachute pants, with yellow vinyl platform sneakers to match.

Like his brothers, however, Zac's largely logo-free, opting not to advertise freebies from such companies as Reebok, Nike, LA Gear, or whatever other sports apparel outfit that may be offering them clothes. On a normal, non-photo-op day, Zac's likely to be in jeans or sweats, V-neck T-shirts, zip-front sweaters and everyday running shoes. So far, he doesn't wear jewelry.

ON THE ASTRO TIP

Because Zac is a Libra (born October 22), one might expect him to be calm and balanced, like the scales representing that sign. But as anyone really familiar with astrology knows, those scales dip up and down several times before reaching that perfect balance. Such is the case with most Libra personalities: Always on the move, first they're up, then they're down. Inconsistency is their most consistent behavior.

Libras love people, but not large noisy crowds. Affable Zac is always open to meeting new people, but he's been seen covering his ears when crowds of them make it too noisy—even if he's the one who coaxed the decibels up.

Libras are usually the peacemakers in the family, but they're also the ones who'll start an argument, just for the fun of it. They're good-natured and pleasant but can also be sulky, especially when expected to just blindly follow orders. If they feel strongly about something, they can be stubborn.

They're also described as bright and cheerful, full of frenzied activity, restless bundles of energy—the perfect description of Zac. So's this: Libras are sweet-expressioned, with a smile that could melt a chocolate bar. They're extremely talky, but they can turn around and be great listeners.

Mostly they're kind, gentle and fair, artistic and very musical. Which sounds a lot like Zac!

LIFE ON THE HOME FRONT

"We love Tulsa!" Ike, Taylor and Zac exclaimed on a morning TV show recently, admitting that they get homesick when they're away for long stretches. Their hometown, however, has displayed somewhat mixed feelings toward them. On the upside, the current governor of Oklahoma, Frank Keating, declared this past May 25 as Hanson Day in the state, honoring the band just as "MMMBop" hit number one on the charts. As it turned out, Hanson couldn't even be there that day to accept the honor: They were in New York City, readying for an appearance on *The David Letterman Show*.

But it wouldn't be surprising if Ike, Taylor and Zac felt a little ambivalent about their new status as hometown heroes. Tulsa's a toddlin' music town, all right, but Hanson music never really set their hometown on fire—not back when they could have used the support, anyway. When the Hanson brothers were playing all around the area, doing everything in their power to get popular, they never quite made it into the Tulsa bigs.

Of course, they probably shouldn't take that one personally. As Janet Robinson of SRO Productions, a Tulsa talent agency, puts it, "Tulsa artists are downplayed in their own hometown. Leon Russell [a veteran blues and rock star], for example, charges more to play Tulsa because he gets more respect around the rest of the country than he does in his own hometown!"

Indeed, according to one of the organizers of Mayfest, in the early '90s, no talent agents could quite figure out what to do with the Hanson Brothers and declined to take them on as clients. Larry Briggs, owner of Tulsa's premier rock arena, the Cain Ballroom, confirms that Hanson never grew popular enough to play at bigger venues. Even the city's main rock music radio station, KTTZ, admits to being among the last to play "MMMBop" this year. As stations all around the U.S.A. jumped on it before its official release, Tulsa's did not.

And when the single was sold out around the rest of the country, there were plenty of available copies in Hanson's hometown. "Tulsans are just weird, I guess," concluded an Internet Tulsa reporter.

The local newspaper writeups about Hanson often displayed more surprise than praise when the band actually did make it. One article in the *Tulsa World* expressed major disbelief: "I thought I was [hallucinating] when I heard that these cherubic, largely ignorable local whimsies had not only landed a major label deal but had hooked up with the Dust Brothers to produce it!" The same article also contained begrudging praise. *"Middle of Nowhere* is the kind of tight, slick record that will beat us over the head for years to come." Talk about a left-handed compliment!

Still, Hanson bears no ill will toward those Tulsans who did not believe in them way back when. They're not the I-told-you-so types. Besides, the family has a deep-rooted allegiance to the town.

Their neighborhood straddles the fence between the rustic and the cookie-cutter suburban referred to in their song "Weird." It's not rural enough to fall into the former category and not nearly tractlike enough to fall into the latter. As one observer has wryly noted, "There is clearly no neighborhood association collecting dues for fancy signs or other such extras. Homes here have few trappings or crafty decor." Still, the nabe is far from ramshackle. Homes, which are not at all uniform, are spaced comfortably apart, with yards large enough to accommodate playing fields for the kids. Indeed, the Hanson backyard sports a soccer goal.

The place the Hanson boys call home is neat but nondescript, quiet and roomy, on a street that slopes downward toward the city line. Out front in the driveway, a few sport-utility vehicles are parked; bales of hay are lined up at intervals in the gully alongside the road to slow down the fast-draining downpours. Thick foliage abounds. The boys have said their house sits on two and a half treed, hilly acres, with several nearby creeks for the kids to run through. When they were younger, they spent quite a bit of time in their very own treehouse. "We built it in the backyard," Zac explains.

Inside, the Hanson home is neat, clean and organized—but far from formal. A long time ago the three oldest boys sort of spread out. "We basically took over the entire house, including the living room," Taylor told a TV audience.

A visiting journalist confirms: "Everywhere you look, there are instruments, sheet music, lyrics scribbled on paper, magazines: their home is their studio. The house is clearly devoted to the kids; it's a place where they can practice and express themselves musically."

And practice they do, even now, up to four hours a day. Naturally, the boys want to improve on their instruments, write new songs and perfect what has always been their signature sound: those heavenly Hanson harmonies.

The oldest boys are responsible for helping with the housework, as they have always been. All the kids have chores to do, including washing the dishes and mowing the lawn, and—reality check—having a number-one record doesn't get Ike, Taylor or Zac out of those! "We don't get special treatment at home," Ike said in an interview.

Taylor adds, "If that ever happens, someone needs to hit us really hard!" Clearly, the Hanson brothers neither want nor expect to be changed by fame.

Right now there are no pets in the Hanson home. "We've had pets that have come and gone," Taylor says.

"We once had six cats," Zac informed a reporter. "But that was because the mother gave birth to a litter of five."

Naturally, the brothers do have a huge contingent of friends and family on their home turf. The boys' younger siblings have been kept out of the spotlight, but all three are close with Ike, Taylor and Zac.

Sisters Jessica (Jessi) and Avery (nicknamed Avie) are eight and six years old; brother Mackenzie, called Mac (yes, it rhymes with Zac) is three. All three are blond.

The older Hanson boys have written songs for each of their siblings. "Funny Bunny" is about Jessi; "Baby Avie" is a rap about Avery. They debuted both the song and the tiniest baby at 1994's Mayfest when their dad joined them onstage holding the then-newborn Mackenzie, as the boys sang "Mackey Baby."

Naturally, the singing sibs are often asked if there's a younger musical Hanson contingent on the horizon. So far, Ike, Tay and Zac have been noncommittal. "They're an artsy crew, all very outgoing in their own way, and definitely have the music in them," Taylor has conceded, "but they'll probably do their own thing."

Zac, however, isn't so sure. As he mentioned to *Rolling Stone* magazine, "Mackie has the rhythm. I've got to watch out. He'll steal my place!"

Jessica, Avery and Mackenzie are certainly getting

a bird's-eye view of all the phenomenal Hanson happenings. Just as the family used to do when the boys were getting started, they continue to travel everywhere together. Sharp-eyed Hanson fans can spot the tiny trio on the sidelines wherever the boys appear. At NBC's *Today* show, a photographer who spotted the younger kids asked if they'd pose with their famous bros: Jessi, Avie and Mac seemed willing, but Mom and Dad stepped in to politely scotch the potential photo op.

In fact, the Hanson boys' parents are even more active in their sons' careers than ever before. It only makes sense: There's more to deal with now that the boys are stars, and more to be wary of. "We never dreamed it would lead to this," their dad confided to a friend. But since it has, like all good parents, Walker and Diana have had to become even more protective of their sons. Unlike some stage parents, they aggressively put the boys' health and welfare before career concerns. During a photo shoot and interview for a magazine in London, Ike, Tay and Zac were asked to pose for pix rollerblading in the grueling heat for several hours, then immediately whisked indoors to a chilly air-conditioned room for an interview. Walker Hanson was reportedly concerned about the boys' catching colds and requested that the location for the interview be switched. Dad wasn't being overly cautious, either: As he mentioned to his friend, Taylor did, in fact, get sick.

As a family, the Hansons seem to be universally well liked and well regarded by their Tulsa friends and associates. "They're an unusual family," says a

Mayfest organizer, "a strong, religious family, really close and really solid. They're more concerned that their kids are having fun and not getting burnt out than about their careers."

Another friend adds, "They're strong, principled, polite people, they've raised kids who are gracious, good-hearted, stable and centered. The Hanson brothers are really great role models. You couldn't find better role models for today's kids than those kids."

Jarrod Gollihare, a longtime family friend, music consultant (he's a musician, and the family would often ask his advice when purchasing a new instrument or perfecting a sound) and journalist, puts it this way: "They are the nicest kids I've ever met in my life. They come from an extremely centered, intelligent, spiritual family. They are polite and friendly, and it's easy to strike up a conversation with them." Clearly, Hanson has its enthusiastic supporters at home.

Home, of course, is where Ike, Tay and Zac's closest friends are. Some are from the neighborhood; many are the kids of fellow employees in their dad's company. None of them, Tay tells, are surprised at or jealous of Hanson's super success. "They've always known this was a part of our life. This is not a shock to them."

"Besides," Ike notes, "we've done music with our friends also. My best friend is in a band."

When Ike, Tay and Zac left home to go to Los Angeles to record their album, their best buds gave them a very special gift: a paperweight globe of Tulsa to remind them of home. The boys take it with them everywhere.

And when they do get home—albeit less and less frequently now—the first thing they do is call their friends. Ike told *MTV News* that the way he wanted to celebrate Hanson reaching number one was by having a big party with all his hometown buds. Zac, ever the comedian, added that he planned to celebrate by "getting a girlfriend." But that's getting ahead of our story!

Most of their friends are home-schooled like Ike, Tay and Zac are, and they frequently get together on educational field trips their parents have designed. No one in Hanson feels he's missed out by not being in a regular classroom; in fact, the boys feel quite the opposite. "I don't think we could be a band without home-schooling," Zac told *16* magazine.

Ike and Taylor explain how it works: "Our parents have been our main teachers, though we've had a tutor recently. You can get a curriculum where you pretty much read the lesson. It'll tell you, 'Read this, now do this.' It's pretty specific."

Of course, as the old expression goes, "All work and no play makes Johnny a dull boy"—but there's nothing dull about any Hanson. While the boys don't have as much leisure time as they used to, they make the most of it when they're (as the famous Leon Russell song goes) "livin' on Tulsa time."

While they deliberately try to keep a low profile at home, Taylor says, "We like to rollerblade, play speed hockey and basketball. Plus Zac and I both draw." The boys also hang at the virtual-reality arcade (Laserquest is Zac's favorite game), listen to all kinds of music, including the classic oldies that inspired them in the first place, and every once in a while they grab a bite at a favorite haunt, like Rex's Boneless Chicken or McDonald's. They also admit a new appreciation for doing simple things they used to take for granted. "Sitting down and doing nothing!" is what Taylor dreams of doing at home. "Sleeping, as much as possible!" adds Ike. They're only half kidding: Their schedule *has* gotten a lot more hectic (!!) in recent months.

Indeed, even when the Hanson boys are home, they have to devote huge chunks of time to practicing and rehearsing. Which means the people they're really around most of the time are each other. Which could conceivably lead to getting on each other's nerves—but Hanson says no, that doesn't happen.

"We're best friends, we don't get in each other's hair," Taylor asserts. Isaac backs him up: "We're brothers and we enjoy each other's company." Okay, sometimes an occasional argument gets sparked, or Zac will do something just to be annoying—like slow down or speed up the pace on his drums while they're in the middle of a song—but that's rare. In fact, the boys feel that they're even *better* friends now than they used to be. "We get in way less arguments now than before," Ike realized recently. "We just get along really well. We have no problems."

LIVIN' LARGE

The hearts of Hanson may be at home in Tulsa, but physically, the boys have been all over the world, in some countries more than once, during the last whirlwind year. They've been back and forth to New York on countless occasions, and they even admit to considering Los Angeles "a second home." That feeling seemed mutual when, during an appearance at L.A.'s Universal Citywalk, Hanson was welcomed back like conquering heroes. "Eardrum piercing, glass-shattering screams," is how the L.A. *Times* described the fifteen hundred delirious fans who showed up to get a glimpse of the trio.

Because they lived in four different countries when they were kids, Ike, Tay and Zac aren't as blown away by foreign travel as they might be. Ike was described as "blasé" when he ticked off recent jaunts to Germany, England and Japan for a reporter. "We spent ten days in the U.K., five in France, three in Germany doing interviews with different magazines, TV and radio stations. We've lived all over the world, so the travel we get to do now is fun, but it's not like we've never done it before."

Okay, maybe he sounded a tad jaded, but the truth is, he and his brothers love being on the road. "It's the best part of what we're doing," Taylor tells us. "Just goin' around seein' the world, goin' all over the country. It's really fun."

Certainly, "the road" loves 'em right back. During one trip to Europe, even before *Middle of Nowhere* was released, Hanson caused a near cyber-riot when an on-line chat session had to be terminated because of the overwhelming volume of hits from fans. As Ike mentioned, they chatted and performed on TV shows, plus posed and answered questions for several foreign fan mags, including such biggies as *Bravo* in Germany and *Smash Hits* in the U.K.

What's the best place they've been to so far? Ike, Tay and Zac are diplomatic about that one, but New York, in the good old U.S.A., seems to have a slight edge. "We've seen a lot of cool places, but every place has its own thing. We really enjoyed being in New York. We had a whole two-day tour, we walked up the steps of the Statue of Liberty," Taylor described enthusiastically. They also hung out at a virtual-reality video arcade in Times Square.

Ike marveled, "New York was a cool experience. Everything is so tall, and it's all in this tiny area."

Of course, the Hanson boys were not exactly your

hanson

Ike, Tay and Zac say "cheese" for the cameras in
Los Angeles.

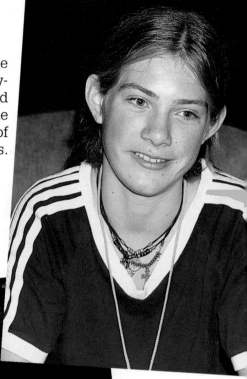

Taylor's the accessory-charged Hanson—he wears lots of chokers.

Taylor comes out of his shell in performance, urging everyone to sing along.
(Photo by Karen Zilch Nadalin)

Tay's the dreamer of the family.
(Photo by Karen Zilch Nadalin)

hanson

ha

Zac's a
maniac on
the drums!
*(Photo by Karen
Zilch Nadalin)*

Signing autographs for lucky fans is important
to the band—they never say no.

You never know what Zac will say or do next!

Self-taught on guitar, Ike's an amazing musician.

Hanson meets the press! The boys are never shy when talking about their music: they love making it! *(Photo by Karen Zilch Nadalin)*

hanson

Ike's been called "the serious one," but he really has quite a zany side.

hanson

All-Access Passes: this book is yours! Tay, Zac and Ike display theirs!

average New York City sightseers when they visited last May. Doing the tourist bit had to be squeezed in between TV appearances, photo sessions and marathon interviews. During one head-spinning week in May, Ike, Tay and Zac were everywhere: total media darlings. Which gave their fans everywhere the perfect opportunity to get to know these darlings just a little better.

A WEEK IN THE PROMOTIONAL LIFE OF HANSON: FROM ROSIE TO REEGE TO KATIE, DAVE AND JENNY . . . AND MORE!

The idea was to kick off the album, already powered, of course, by the comet "MMMBop." To that end, Hanson flew to New York, holed up in the über-cool Rhiga Royal Hotel (where all the rock stars stay) and did back-to-back TV chat shows, interviews and photo sessions with the top echelon of the entertainment press.

Their days began early and ended late. They sang "MMMBop" dozens of times and answered the same exact questions ("How'd you get started?" "Do you really write your own music?" "What's 'MMMBop' about?") dozens upon *dozens* of times. Never once did any Hanson get cranky or fail to respond enthusiastically—as if that was the first time anyone had asked that question. Now *that* takes work!

The whirlwind week that was began with what was intended to be a low-key appearance at Paramus

Park Mall in New Jersey. Sponsored by top radio station Z-100, the plan was for Hanson to perform two songs on a crudely erected stage in the middle of the food court, then field a question-and-answer session moderated by deejay Cubby Bryant. The appearance was not heavily promoted, and "MMMBop," though being played on the radio, hadn't even hit the charts yet. In other words, no one expected more than a thousand fans, tops, to show up. The mall itself isn't particularly large; the second-floor food court area is minuscule by most shopping mall standards. Hanson was scheduled to appear around eight o'clock.

The radio station and mall security should have had a clue that things would not go as expected when, as early as noon, fans began showing up to claim primo spots. Waves of fans, one after another, many with their moms, continued all day long: by five, every escalator, elevator and stairway up to the food court had to be cordoned off. Overflow fans were stuck downstairs, without hope of even a view of Hanson. Extra security had to be called in.

By seven, that estimate of one thousand had reached six thousand—Hanson fans had come from near and far and overtaken the mall. All were in high spirits, demonstrated by high-pitched screaming whenever the name "Hanson" was dropped by the deejay. "No one has seen anything like this before," exclaimed a befuddled shopkeeper. "It's bedlam, like the second coming of the Osmonds!"

Indeed, by the time Hanson did show up—

around eight-thirty—the fans had jammed every mall entrance, and the boys had to be surrounded by bodyguards and spirited up by employee elevator to the food court. The enthusiasm of Hanson fans was demonstrated by glass-shattering hysteria—a response for which Ike, Tay and Zac, for all their worldliness, were totally unprepared. Zac actually covered his ears as he was guided onto the stage by bodyguards.

As Isaac later described it to *Newsweek,* "The place was mobbed, more than [the crowds at] Christmas!"

"It was pretty crazy," Zac added. "We were nervous because previously, the biggest crowd we'd played in front of was a couple of hundred, maybe, not 6,000!"

Taylor explained, "[In that situation] you're not nervous about singing in front of everyone—you're nervous for your life!"

At times, it did seem as if the surging crowd would break through the barriers (some were only duct tape—that's how unprepared the mall was) and rush Hanson. But in the end, fans gave the band its props and sang along joyfully as Ike, Tay and Zac performed "MMMBop," and "Where's the Love?" Ike played guitar with an assist from a backup musician and urged the crowd, 'Let's rock 'n' roll!'; Taylor shook the tambourine, while Zac kept the beat with handheld castanets.

Hanson gave it their best shot, but in the end, the boys had to be rushed out after ten minutes.

The question-and-answer session was scotched: The noise level was out of bounds, and record company execs decided that no one would be heard anyway.

What Ike, Tay and Zac heard, when they had time to reflect, was the beginning of real Hanson-mania. The brothers were juiced beyond their wildest dreams. It was really happening.

It happened over and over again that entire week, as Hanson met and charmed often cynical journalists from *Entertainment Weekly, Rolling Stone, Spin,* The *New York Times, 16, Teen Beat, Time, Time for Kids, Newsweek* and *New York Daily News.* They posed for day-long photo sessions for *Seventeen* and *Interview* magazine.

And then they did TV—did they ever! First came *The Rosie O'Donnell Show.* The Emmy Award-winning chat fest rivals only *Oprah!* as the most-watched daytime talk show. Maybe that's why Hanson seemed just the slightest bit nervous. They performed first. Bolstered by a trio of backup musicians, each boy played his instrument and urged the audience to clap along to "MMMBop."

Ike, Tay and Zac relaxed perceptibly as pop-culture princess Rosie, who clearly knows a teen phenom when she sees one, dubbed them "Cutie patooties . . . a TV series waiting to happen." While becoming a new generation Partridge Family doesn't exactly top Hanson's wish list, savvy Ike promised Rosie a backstage pass to Hanson's first full-scale concert.

"Baptized" by the Rosie O'Donnell experience, Hanson went on to NBC's *Today* show, where they performed outdoors at New York's famous Rockefeller Plaza. Ike described the experience as "totally awesome." They also chatted with anchor Katie Couric, who proclaimed them "a band sure to make teen hearts beat a little faster." The perky morning hostess attempted to coax Hanson siblings Jessi, Avie and Mac onstage, but without success. "They're a little camera shy," Taylor explained politely.

Hanson went over the same performing-and-chatting territory on *The CBS Morning News.* There they took the opportunity to remind a national audience that *Middle of Nowhere* is actually their third album, after the two independents they did. "Aren't they darling?" gushed the anchor of that show.

Next, Ike, Tay and Zac did lengthy on-camera interviews with *MTV News,* VH-1 and MTV's *The Week in Rock,* followed by *The Jenny McCarthy Show.* "Jenny was fun," Taylor ventured, echoing many a teenage boy's perception of the sexy and zany performer.

The band was blown away, however, when they were invited on *The David Letterman Show,* which they consider the pinnacle of cool. As Zac expressed, "It's Letterman! It's like, whoa, why would Letterman want us? But if he wants us, I'll go!"

Go they did, and performed as well. The boys didn't even seem miffed that Dave was the only one who didn't invite them for a sit-down. Instead, the quirky-cool host came over and shook hands with everyone, including their backup musicians, asking each, "Are you a Hanson?"

Ike, Tay and Zac were TV pros by the time they settled in for a fairly in-depth chat with Regis and Kathie Lee on their mega-popular morning show, *Live*. Smoothly and politely, they answered questions about how it felt having a number-one song, what they used to squabble about and how they could write about subjects they have yet to experience, like love.

The boys performed two songs "unplugged"— that is, without backup. The harmonies were silky and tight, as Taylor, tambourine in hand, led off with the plaintive "ooh, oohs" of "MMMBop." Ike played guitar, while Zac clicked the castanets. They wrapped the show with an unplugged, albeit abbreviated, version of "Madeline," on which Taylor and Ike traded off lead vocals.

After a week like that, you'd think Hanson would be "MMMBop"-ed and talked out, but not even. As soon as they finished the last interview, they hopped a trans-Atlantic flight to start a three-week European promo jaunt.

Then Hanson returned to the United States, to appear on *The Tonight Show with Jay Leno* and debut as presenters at the MTV movie awards in Los Angeles. They spent the rest of the month back on the promo-go-round, stopping in Detroit, Oklahoma City, Charlotte and Minneapolis. In July, they were off to Southeast Asia.

Is it any wonder Ike, Tay and Zac fantasize about sleeping when they get home?

HANSON IN YOUR HOMETOWN: THE TOUR!

Of course, there's a difference between traveling and being on tour—lately, all the traveling hit-making Hanson has done has been for promotional purposes. They've made pit stops in various places for press conferences, TV guest shots and mini-concerts to give fans and the media a taste of what's ahead. The best—a full-blown tour—is yet to come.

Hanson fans cannot wait.

For as any true fan knows, reading about Ike, Tay and Zac in 'zines and newspapers is cool; seeing the band on TV is better; but nothing beats the up-close and personal experience of seeing them live and in person in your hometown.

Hanson thinks so too. "We would love to tour soon," Taylor told MTV. "It's kinda a bummer that we don't get to play all the time, but we're practicing. I mean, we've never really done a full-scale tour before. We've been doing local gigs for a long time. We did three hundred performances in five years."

Ike puts it this way: "Seeing all the people, all the kids who come to see us play, that's a pretty great feeling. We definitely miss performing for people. It's a ton of fun to perform."

Zac adds, "We're not nervous at all—we can't wait to get out and do it!"

So, is it going to happen? And if so, when? Where? And how can a fan increase his or her chances of meeting them? Read on.

* * *

When they may tour: Ike, for one, has been careful not to give Hanson fans false hope. "A tour will depend on how the album does," he says. Meaning: If for some unfathomable reason, *Middle of Nowhere* tanks, the group would not tour solely on the strength of "MMMBop." One hit record does not a tour support, and Ike's savvy enough to know that.

However, *Middle of Nowhere* did not tank, not by a long shot. It hit the Top 10 its first week out and climbed from there. Further, the success of Hanson's second single, "Where's the Love?" proved the band is no "one-hit blunder," as one newspaper snidely put it.

Therefore, a Hanson tour would appear to be in the bag, soon.

The only hitch: A delay would only be caused by the time it takes to put together a rockin' show. They'll need staging, backup musicians, choreography, the whole shebang. After all, if Hanson fans are going to pay to see them, Hanson will make sure fans get their money's worth.

Where they'll tour: Expect a Hanson tour to take them all across the U.S.A. and Canada. No doubt they'll hit all major cities—New York, Chicago, L.A., Miami, Detroit, Boston, Cleveland, Toronto, Vancouver—and lots of smaller ones too. After they do North America, Europe and Asia will be next.

The only hitch: Because Hanson got so popular so fast, many venues may not have room for them on already-packed schedules that were booked months in advance. Therefore, the first time out, Hanson may play in whatever cities can accommodate them.

And Tulsa, too? Their hometown posse—including those who pretty much ignored them just a year ago—would naturally love to have Hanson back. The owner of the Blue Rose Café has just opened another restaurant, where he's hoping Hanson will play. However, even the band's earliest supporters and close personal friends realize that probably won't happen. It's doubtful Ike, Tay and Zac could go back to playing elementary schools, churches, water parks and restaurants. Mayfest? Maybe—on the main stage, this time.

What to expect onstage: Just because Hanson is new to the charts hardly makes them novice performers. They've been hop-scotching the heartland for the past five years, and though it's been on a much smaller scale, they *do* know how to rock the house! Ike, Tay and Zac are not just going to get up onstage and sing, cool as that might be. You can bet the boys will do some serious dancing, animated byplay and spring some surprises on their audience. All three will certainly do more talking than simply introducing each song. Taylor will probably urge the crowd to "scream as loud as you can." Of course, *he'll* probably be wearing earplugs. As for Zac— well, forewarned is forearmed. There's no telling what he might do in concert.

Ike, Tay and Zac don't have a definite song lineup just yet, but they do plan to include some oldies along with *Middle of Nowhere* tracks. "It's always fun when you play songs that the audience gets into," Taylor dished to MTV. "So hopefully, we'll put some of those [oldies from the '50s and '60s] into our show to add some flavor."

Isaac agrees: "Yeah, we definitely want to do that. You can say that kind of music is 'dear to us' because it was very inspirational."

Zac quips, "It *is* dear to us—like Rudolph!"

Fearless Prediction: They'll open with the rollicking "Where's the Love?" and end their set with the swayable "I Will Come to You." Candles will be lit.

Not-So-Fearless Prediction: Any Hanson live show will have built-in riot potential. The band is that hot—and that cute. This warning, posted on one of the many Hanson Internet sites, puts it best: "Please, do not attack the band! Make the live experience fun for everyone. Respect the band."

What to expect offstage: The entire Hanson family will no doubt be with Ike, Tay and Zac. They've always traveled together, always put family first, above all else. Just because they're mega-stars, that won't change.

Tutors, too, will travel with Hanson this time. At sixteen, fourteen and eleven, the boys still have to go to school. Being mega-stars doesn't change that, nor would any of the guys want it too. They know the importance of a formal education, and all three want to graduate high school on time. The chaos of being on the road may, however, make it difficult for Mr. and Mrs. Hanson to do all the necessary teaching, so extra edu-help will come in handy.

Like most rockers on the road, Hanson will probably travel in a caravan of deluxe tour buses, equipped with all the amenities of home: kitchen, bunk beds, bathroom, den, TV, VCR, stereo and phones. Neat as those mobile homes might be, the boys won't spend all their nights aboard them. They'll no doubt be holed up in deluxe hotels in each town they visit. Which leads to . . .

All access—a fan's best chance of meeting them: If you love Hanson, you're in great company. Hanson fans were first to pick up on them, flood radio station request lines, MTV call-ins and, of course, the Net. All Hanson fans want to meet the guys; smart Hanson fans have the best shot.

The first, most important, step is to find out when they're coming to your town.

That's best accomplished several ways.

Listen to the radio station in your town that plays Hanson. They'll have the most up-to-date, accurate info on the where and when of a Hanson stopover. Even better, radio stations often have promotional meet-the-band contests. No fan wants to miss out on those. Someone's got to win, might as well be you.

Check teen magazines, which may have tour dates listed, but don't neglect your local newspaper, which may be more on top of last-minute gigs.

Calling up potential venues is not a bad idea either. Wherever rockers normally play in your area—an arena, stadium, theater—chances are Hanson could be booked there too.

The Internet: The electronic grapevine is as fast as it gets—only problem is, it's not always accurate. Most of the Hanson sites are designed by fans, many of whom don't have any more info than you do. However, the official Hanson site should have accurate information, as should the one maintained by Mercury Records. For the addresses of both, see the "Where to Reach Hanson" section at the end of this book.

Once you've figured out when Hanson's coming to town and where they'll be playing, you can increase your chances of "bumping into them" in several ways. The best is via a promotional setup with a radio station. Before each concert, all bands normally do what's called a meet-and-greet. That is, special time is put aside backstage for the band to personally shake hands with fans, pose for photos and sign autographs. Most of the lucky fans who participate are radio station contest winners.

Representatives from local newspapers and magazines are generally invited to interview bands that are performing in town. Sometimes that includes at least one intrepid reporter from a school newspaper. Now might be a good time to see about staff signups.

Another tip: All bands do what's called a sound check in each city they play at. It involves checking out the venue several hours before show time to be sure all sound, lighting and other techno-concerns are working smoothly. The afternoon of a nighttime gig will surely see the band pull up at the venue, duck in a side door and do their thing. Many fans have met their idols by being in the vicinity of the stage door the afternoon of the show.

Really intrepid fans with really indulgent parents have also had successful encounters with stars by registering at the same hotel the band stays at. It takes research—start with the priciest in town—but it can be done. It *has* been done.

A last resort: networking. Or, as the cliché goes, "It's not what you know, it's who you know." Do you know anyone with connections—to the radio station, the venue, the hotel, city officials, the press most likely to cover Hanson? Do your parents? It can't hurt to ask around.

THE SONG AND THE
VIDEO, FROM "MMMBOP"
TO THE TIPPY TOP!

After all those years of hop-scotching the Midwest, performing at state fairs, neighborhood parties, school assemblies, local clubs and water parks, a ditty dubbed "MMMBop" catapulted Hanson to the top. Some ditty!

The remixed version of "MMMBop," a combination of Isaac, Taylor and Zac's original, plus the Dust Brothers' production, was released by Mercury Records to radio stations—but not stores—on March 24, 1997. A spokesperson for New York City's top-rated WPLJ explained his station's reaction to the song to *Billboard,* a music industry trade magazine: "We played the song two weeks early. It's rare for us to do that, but we had ten [new] records in the stack to listen to in a meeting and that's the one everyone just said, 'Wow!' when they heard it. It sounds like the Jackson 5—you can't understand a word they're saying, but you don't care. It bridges all ages. It's infectious!"

That scenario was repeated at radio stations all around the country. First, the collective, instant "Wow!" from deejays and program directors, then the rush of "Play that again!" calls from listeners. Within days of the "MMMBop" mailing, it became the most requested song on college and Top 40 radio outlets around the country. Which was wonderful and frustrating at the same time: Listeners who were hooked on the song wanted to own it immediately—only it wasn't in stores yet. "That's not an unusual strategy for record companies," says music industry veteran Danny Fields. "They whet listeners' appetites first, building anticipation for the day the single does arrive in the stores. Then everyone rushes out to buy it, and it hits the charts in a high position."

A savvy strategy; still, it can't work unless the song is amazing. Of course, "MMMBop" is, and it did. Early in April, it jumped onto *Billboard's* "Airplay" charts, its first week tracking at number 49 out of 100. "Airplay" is calculated by the electronic monitoring of 312 radio stations around the country, twenty four hours a day, seven days a week. In other words, "MMMBop" got played a lot! The following week, the song jumped to number 34, then to 20, finally hitting number one in early June.

For those first several weeks, it did not appear on the Hot 100 Singles chart at all. But when it did debut, a week after its end-of-April sales release, it hit the charts running: "MMMBop" leapt on at number 16, easily earning itself Hot Shot Debut honors, plus a notation in *Billboard's* Singles Spotlight column. After detailing the song's sensational chart splash, columnist Theda Sandiford-Waller noted, "If you are not already familiar with the teen trio, you will be!"

That was just the beginning. The following week, "MMMBop" jumped to number 6; then number 2. In the May 24, 1997, issue of *Billboard*—three weeks after it hit the stores—"MMMBop" was the number-one song around the country. It also climbed to number one in Casey Kasem's nationally syndicated radio countdown show.

That historic week alone, "MMMBop" sold a reported 140,000 copies. *Billboard* further reported that it was being heard by 50 million people, and of the 161 radio stations monitored, 49 were playing it more than 50 times a week. Just as the WPLJ spokesman predicted, "MMMBop" wasn't for teens only; it also powered its way onto *Billboard's* Adult Top 40 charts, where it hit the top ten in a matter of weeks. A dance version of the tune was released in early June; after being played in clubs, it appeared on dance charts.

The asteroid "MMMBop" didn't just crash onto U.S. charts; in Canada, it hit number one at the same time. In early June, "MMMBop" ruled Europe, Australia and Japan. It's doubtful any listener in those countries understood the words at first: In the grand tradition of instant classics, "MMMBop" proved that music really *is* the universal language.

The stats, while mind-boggling, hardly tell the real story. You can't sing along to stats. You *must* sing, clap, tap, move, groove and bop along to "MMMBop." In fact, you just can't stop. "MMMBop" is pure power pop, a song destined to be programmed into our collective "instant replay consciousness" for decades.

The lyrics refer to "a secret no one knows," but the secret of the song's monster success is no secret at all.

It arrived on the scene at the intersection of Right Place-Right Song-Right Time-Right Artists.

Bouncier than a ping-pong ball in a wind tunnel, catchier than the flu, more uplifting than the perfect date on prom night, sweeter than Taylor's plaintive "oooh, ooohs" that kick it off, "MMMBop" is a swirly pop confection that grabs you from the get-go. "Once heard, never purged," is the way Hanson's official bio puts it. An Internet fan put it this way: "It's cool because you just stop thinking about all the bad stuff around that sad songs remind you of, and you get this happy feeling from it."

Though Taylor's is the plaintive voice singing lead on "MMMBop," the heavenly harmonies achieved by his brothers are the icing on the cake.

But it takes more than a monumentally marvelous song, even when it's strategically set upon the public, to achieve the kind of instant and incredible success "MMMBop" did. Timing plays a major role as well. And "MMMBop" had it goin' on in that department. The song came out just when the music industry most needed a shot in the arm.

There's room for a wide variety of sounds on the musical landscape, but the switch for pure, energizing power pop seemed to be stuck in the OFF position. Instead, the music being played most pervasively in the last few years was a whole lot of alternative, rap, or just really bland: your mother's radio station lite stuff. The hugest artists were typified by the angry, but real, Alanis Morissette, the really angry (and tragically deceased) Tupac Shakur or the really angry, poetic and inscrutable Nirvana, Pearl Jam, Live. Performers like Celine Dion, Toni Braxton and Michael Bolton filled the adult-oriented air waves.

While those forms honestly did reflect the feelings and lifestyles of huge segments of the music-listening population, masses of people *didn't* relate to it at all and didn't buy it. Which led overall record sales to sag, which in turn led panicky movers and shakers frantically searching for the next big thing.

If you listened, you could almost hear the cries of younger, happier 'tweens and teens all across the country: "Enough with mope rock! No more placentas falling on the floor! Enough with violent, anti-girl, gangsta rap! We appreciate that, but some of us are *not* tormented or angry! Give us fun, uncomplicated music we can relate to—and, even better, swoon to!" Perhaps that's overstating it, but no one's arguing there was a niche to be filled in pop music. And along bounced "MMMBop"!

Listeners were first to get it, but the reviewers weren't far behind. "A sunny, vibrant slice of soul pop, reminiscent of classic Jackson 5 stompers like

'ABC' and 'I Want You Back,' detailed one magazine. "Infectious, uplifting, and emotionally charged," said the stuffy *New York Times*. *Billboard's* take on "MMMBop," which it spotlighted as "new and noteworthy," was, "Try to imagine what the Jackson 5 might sound like with the accompaniment of a skittling funk beat and scratchy faux . . . ultimately quite cool . . . a catchy chorus . . . a runaway smash." *Entertainment Weekly* enthused, "['MMMBop'] is an undeniable confection . . . a giddy trampoline bounce of a record . . . it isn't some romper-rock novelty. It's fully realized pop that just happens to be sung by kids." The publication then crowned it "the overdue return of bubblegum pop."

Whew! That's a lot of accolades for one frothy pop confection. How did Isaac, Taylor and Zac react to the landslide of enthusiasm for their composition? Naturally, the boys were psyched, big time—but they were also a little confused. They wondered if anyone listening understood that the feel-good song of summer was kinda . . . sad. It doesn't help, of course, that the lyrics are kinda . . . hard to understand.

So what is it all about? Hanson explains.

"The song is basically about friendship," Isaac states.

Zac says, "It's about holding on to the ones who really care, which might be your brothers and sisters if you have them."

Taylor adds, "MMMBop is a pretty fun song—but deeper than it sounds."

The song says that although we have a lot of friendships and relationships as we go through life, only very few are destined to last. The people you loved, or thought you loved, well, in an "MMMBop"—in other words, in a split second—they could be gone. Which sounds like a downer, but ultimately, the song is inspirational, urging you to stay close to the people who'll really be there for you through thick and thin. And to keep trying, keep forming new relationships—because you never know which will take root and last forever.

"MMMBop" may be about relationships, but its message can be applied to everything you do in life. Keep trying, keep planting those seeds, never give up—because you never know which effort, which flower, will come to fruition. Isaac, Taylor and Zac have *lived* by that message.

A VIDEO VIEW

Like the single, the video for "MMMBop" was an instant smash. It hopped into MTV's Buzz Bin its first week out of the box and from there vaulted up the video charts. Instantly, request lines lit up; there were weeks where it seemed to be on 24/7. It soon hit number one on MTV, MTV-1, VH-1, The Box and became Canada's MuchMusic "Choice Cut" as well.

Unlike the single, however, the video for "MMMBop" didn't have the advantage of being reworked and polished. In fact, as recently as February 1997, there *was* no video at all. During an interview with *16* magazine back then, the boys were asked what they thought an upcoming video would be about. They were quasi-clueless about it.

"We're just looking for a director now," Isaac acknowledged casually.

"We'll find out what's going to be in it when we make the video," Taylor added. "It will depend on the director."

The director Hanson settled on, just a few weeks after that interview, was the Los Angeles–based Tamra Davis. She'd worked with Adam Sandler on the film *Billy Madison* and helmed a rap film called *CB4*. Tamra's résumé also includes directing videos for the bands Sonic Youth, Amp and Luscious Jackson. While Tamra had never worked with a group as young and upbeat as Hanson, she and the band bonded instantly.

"What was really cool about her," Taylor told Jarrod Gollihare of *Urban Tulsa* magazine, "was that she really wanted our input, and wanted to know what we thought. She called us before she told [the record company or anybody else] her ideas for the video. She kinda polished the ideas we'd given her, and put some different things in there. And that's what the video turned out to be."

"There was a lot of creative input on both our parts. It was very much a collaborative effort," Isaac noted.

It was also a very loose, fun shoot that incorporated Hanson's youthful exuberance. "We were just acting weird and [director Davis] would say, 'Just do that in show motion,'" Zac told *Rolling Stone*.

The upshot was "MMMBop," the video. While not a literal retelling of the song—a flower gets planted, but there are no scenes of losing friends or loved ones—it very much captures its spirit of fun and friendship. In a series of fast-paced "MMMBop" moments, it also very much captures the zany spirits of Ike, Taylor and Zac. It's hyperactive, silly in spots, serious in others, a mix of self-conscious and carefree. Just like Hanson! But how much of what's in the video really relates to their lives? And how much of it is just a bunch of props? Here's a quick Hanson video-guide to the personal tidbits that can be gleaned by watching it.

The house and street scenes: No, they're not hometown scenes. The entire video, interiors and exteriors, was shot in Los Angeles.

The taxi, the bus, the Humvee: One of the first images in the video is Ike, Taylor and Zac piling into the back seat of a cab, romping on a city bus, and taking turns behind the wheel of a Humvee—a military Jeeplike vehicle. All of which was *their* idea. Tamra's original suggestion—riding bikes—was squashed by the boys as "too juvenile." Instead, Hanson suggested the taxi, bus and Humvee, which, Taylor tattles, belonged to Sandra Bullock's *Speed 2* character.

Splish-splashing on the beach: While there's not a lot of beach in Oklahoma, there was plenty when the family lived in the Caribbean and South America. The frolicking-on-the-beach part came naturally!

Rollerblading: No need for stunt doubles he[re]—what you see is all Hanson. Blading is one of their favorite activites. The boys wheel around Tulsa all the time and they're quite adept at it. And yes, they elected to leave in the unscripted part where Taylor and Ike crash into one another. "The wipeout was definitely real," Zac admits.

The Einstein poster, the phone booth, the cave: Don't look for deep-rooted symbolism or significance. All were props.

Playing their instruments and singing: No explanation or backing track needed. Ike, Taylor and Zac did really play on the video. And there were no special effects needed to pump up the fun factor; the expressions on their faces tell it all. Hanson loves performing. But only Zac could explain why his hair is braided in some scenes.

What they said when it was finished: "It's just a fun video. There's lots of running around. And there's a part where we sing, 'Plant a seed/plant a flower/plant a rose,' and we throw some seeds down, and a flower grows and we end up [performing] as a band on top of the flower. And then we're bouncing on the moon—and then, we're with Einstein!"

So thrilled was Hanson with the results of the "MMMBop" video, they asked Tamra to direct their next one, "Where's the Love?" They even flew her to England, where they were at the time, to do it.

11

MIDDLE OF NOWHERE

The first major-label Hanson CD, *Middle of Nowhere,* was released to radio stations and stores on May 6, 1997, a scant few months after recording and final mixing was completed. By that time, Hanson's "MMMBop"ping fans were already waiting on line to buy it. And reviewers were already waiting, pens poised, to write about it. The fans weren't disappointed; many reviewers—on the whole, a jaded lot—admitted to being pleasantly surprised.

The reviews for *Middle of Nowhere* were, on balance, pretty good. *Billboard* noted its "relentlessly contagious melodies, uncomplicated lyrics and layered harmonies." The band, the magazine wrote, "seems determined to help steer music away from grunge and back to an unabashedly tuneful sound, reminiscent of early rock 'n' roll. Refresh-

ingly, Isaac, Taylor and Zac Hanson are tale.
singer/songwriters."

The *New York Post* hailed *Middle of Nowhere* as "a bright, uptempo disc" and went on to favorably compare it with classics sung by teen stars of yester-year: "as authentic as the teen tunes by Phil and Don Everly, as heartfelt and pure as the love songs of Richie Valens." The newspaper gave Issac and Zac a special thumbs-up: "Ike's guitar lessons have paid off—he has an excellent range that can get the music to turn and churn with a steady Motown chugga-chugga. And Zac is a real surprise."

Entertainment Weekly called the record "utterly natural and unaffected—yummy!" and rated it an A-.

Canada's *Calgary-Sun* put it concisely: *"Middle of Nowhere* is not a good teenybopper album—it's a good album. Period."

Only *Time* magazine begged to differ. Lumping Hanson in with young musicians Radish and Jonny Lang, *Time* trashed all three, tagging their efforts "immature, mediocre albums that are as much fun as a wet sandbox."

Hanson fans didn't really need to read the reviews. Most had already made their decision about *Middle of Nowhere* and snapped up copies of the CD and/or cassette as soon as it went on sale. Selling 72,000 copies that very first week, Hanson's debut major-label album hit the charts at an amazing number 9, the highest-charting debut that week. One Internet fan summed up the feelings of most Hanson lovers: *"Middle of Nowhere* rocks!"

* * *

Because Isaac, Taylor and Zac really are young, and because their music is original, the songs they write reflect the feelings and concerns people their age can relate to. Which doesn't mean Hanson has actually experienced every situation in every song. They're talented enough to imagine what certain situations would feel like, put it to words and music and, in doing so, touch each and every listener's heart. Ironically, the album is called *Middle of Nowhere,* but its themes are truly universal.

Here's the track-by-track inside track.

Track 1: "Thinking of You"

Written by: Ike, Taylor and Zac.

Lead singer: Taylor. His voice mirrors the feelings in the song, flipping between the yearning for someone you can't have and positively soaring as the imagery of his fantasies takes over.

Tempo: Mid-tempo. "It feels like a bike ride with a pal on a sunny spring day," described *Entertainment Weekly.*

Dance/Clap-o-Meter: It's no "MMMBop," but you can and will move. Score: 8 out of 10.

Weep/Sap-o-Meter: It's sad, but the optimism of the "when" outweighs the sadness of the "now." Score: 7.

Major theme: A love that has to wait.

What they say: It was a cinch to write. Taylor told *MTV News,* "We were just jammin' together, and that song started flowing in—thirty minutes later it was written! That's a weird example of how suddenly a song can come together."

Storyline: "Thinking of You" is about a b̶
yearning to hook up with the girl of his dreams but
can't. He's forced to be stranded outside the fence
of her home, beyond her heart. Why? The song
doesn't say, exactly. It doesn't need to; that way,
each listener can bring his or her own experiences
to it. Maybe the couple in the song is too young;
maybe their parents are against the relationship;
maybe they just come from different worlds and
can't bridge the societal gap. No matter, the boy
knows he was meant to be with this girl. It's all he
thinks about, all day, all night, dreaming of the
time they can finally be a couple—and, on the
wings of love, fly high and break free of everything
that's keeping them apart.

Who will relate: Anyone who has ever been kept
away from the boy/girl of her/his dreams.

Track 2: "MMMBop"

For the MMM-IN-depth, see the previous chapter.

Track 3: "Weird"

Written by: The Hanson brothers and Desmond
Child.

Lead singer: Taylor. The plaintive pain in his
voice is startling.

Tempo: Power ballad.

Dance/Clap-o-Meter: It's *the* slow dance on the
album. Swaying, yes; clapping? Nah. Score: 2.

Weep/Sap-o-Meter: High—a true heart-wrencher. Hanson moves you with a weeper as easily as they grooved you with an "MMMBop"-er. Score: 9.

Major theme: Not fitting in.

What they say: "We were trying to think of interesting ideas for a song," says Ike. "We'd been talking about the word 'weird.'"

Taylor adds, "Talking about the fact that nobody had ever written a song about 'weird.' It seemed strange to us."

"'Cause you use it so much," explains Ike.

"Yeah, think about how many times a day you say 'weird'! So we just took that word and wrote a song, just started playing chords," explains Taylor.

"In the studio with Desmond Child, we started throwing out ideas," Ike says, "melody lines, different lyrics, things like that. Certain things stuck. That song came together very quickly. It's one of those songs that just flowed, and we basically just came up with it in several hours. Certain songs happen fast, and that was one of them. It was very much a mood thing."

Storyline: The mood is haunting. A thoughtful, gripping ballad, it's about feeling so alone, in so many ways, and being stuck in a place where no one understands. The world is about conformity, and if you don't fit in—but aren't different enough to really stand out—it's devastating. Especially when you know that, like everyone else, you deserve that place in the sun. "Weird," in fact, is about yearning not to be so alone, but it includes everyone: At different times in our lives, don't we all long to ~ in?

Who will relate: Anyone who's ever felt like a wallflower, too average to be noticed, yet too weird to be included; anyone who's ever been teased, who's ever bid for attention but couldn't get it. In other words—probably everyone, at one point or another.

Track 4: "Speechless"

Written by: Lyrics by Hanson; music by Hanson and Steve Lironi.

Lead singer: Taylor.

Tempo: Midtempo, with a skate funk, "wah-wah" bass line.

Dance/Clap-o-Meter: Not a classic dance song, but you can move. Score: 6.

Weep/Sap-o-Meter: Bad things are happening, but you won't cry. Score: 0.

Major theme: Knowing you're about to get dumped.

What's been said: It captures the old Motown rockin' energy.

Storyline: She's betraying him. When confronted, she refuses to be honest, but her body language and the way she talks behind his back—all the telltale signs are there. He knows he's about to be dumped, but she won't admit it. He wants her to just be honest and be done with it! And so they're both speechless: She's sneaky; he's furious, rendered speechless by his anger. And he wonders if she ever loved him in the first place, or if the whole relationship was just some sort of game to her. Maybe they don't really know each other at all; that's what happens when you don't communicate, when you're speechless.

Who will relate: Anyone who has ever been betrayed by a boyfriend or girlfriend.

Track 5: "Where's the Love?"

Written by: Mark Hudson, Ike, Taylor and Zac.

Lead singer: Taylor, but Ike forcefully takes over on the song's bridge verses.

Tempo: Supercharged! The hardest rocker on the album, it's also the group's second single.

Dance/Clap-o-Meter: This one's a toe-tapping rocker. Score: 9.

Weep/Sap-o-Meter: More confrontational than sad. Score: 2.

Major theme: Too much fighting, not enough making up.

What they say: Songwriter Mark Hudson brought the concept to Hanson and reveals that, at first, the boys were not into this song. "They resisted it because they felt it was too much of a pop song, and after 'MMMBop,' were afraid they'd be categorized as just another pop act." But Mark urged them to "just try it," and the rest is history. "Where's the Love?" is considered one of the best, most popular songs on the album.

Storyline: A boy and girl love each other, but she's selfish, she wants it her way all the time. And so they fight, 24-7, going back and forth with the same tired arguments. He knows it shouldn't be like this; love shouldn't be this hard. And he wonders if it's worth holding on to such a fractious relationship without the TLC.

Who will relate: Anyone who's been in a brutal, bickering relationship.

Track 6: "Yearbook"

Written by: The Hansons and veteran songwriter Ellen Shipley.

Lead singer: Taylor; but your parents might say it sounds a lot like the young Michael Jackson—it's very soulful.

Tempo: Basically a power ballad with a long piano intro, it moves between slow and uptempo.

Dance/Clap-o-Meter: You can move, but this one's more for listening. Score: 2.

Weep/Sap-o-Meter: More chilling than sad, really, but still, fairly high. Score: 8.

Major theme: Losing a friend, losing a piece of your past.

What they say: Even though Ike, Taylor and Zac have never been to a school, and hence probably don't have a yearbook, this song was inspired by just looking through one.

"Originally, the song was called 'Johnny,'" Ike says, "and it's really a cool song because it's got an interesting meaning behind it. It came about one day when we were talking about a yearbook."

Taylor continues: "A lot of times in a yearbook,

there's a space for a photo but there is none. It just says 'photo unavailable,' because someone didn't get their picture in. That song was just built on that thought."

Storyline: One year after graduation, a boy is flipping through his high-school yearbook. Inexplicably, he becomes obsessed by the one photo that isn't there. Not that he ever cared before, but it suddenly becomes crucial to find out why. What happened to Johnny? Maybe Johnny just wasn't around on photo day; maybe he died; maybe he's someone who "lived in the shadows" that no one really knew. He's determined to find out what happened—and he believes people know but won't say. The boy feels regretful, mourning the loss of someone he didn't know but perhaps should have. Worse, he's haunted by the thought that he and his classmates did something to cause Johnny's disappearance.

Who will relate: Hanson's older fans, who've maybe even experienced that tinge of regret and a sudden, desperate need to know what happened, not only to a person but to a life left behind.

Track 7: "Look at You"

Written by: Lyrics by Hanson; music by Hanson and Stephen Lironi.

Lead singer: Taylor.

Tempo: Uptempo: a swirling, twirling, pounding dance-o-rama of a song.

Dance/Clap-o-Meter: Put your dancin' shoes on,

'cause this one cranks it up and takes it to the floor. Score: 9.

Weep/Sap-o-Meter: There's a bit of yearning to come out of the shadows and into the spotlight, but mostly it's upbeat. Score: 3.

Major theme: She's the superstar; he's admiring from afar.

Listen for: Though Taylor's out front in the lead, Zac comes in at the end, doing his "turn me loose, like a long-necked goose" rendition of James Brown.

Storyline: Although "Look at You" is a straight-ahead dance song, it does tell a story. It's a hard-rock ode to a high-school sex symbol. All eyes are on the girl in the middle of the dance floor. She's the sizzling superstar, completely at home in the spotlight, effortlessly making it her own. The wallflower boy is so uncomfortable there, he just wishes he could disappear. Until, that is, she turns and spots him squirming uncomfortably in the shadows. She extends her hand and coaxes him out of his shell and into her world. Fantasy fulfilled!

Who will relate: Sometimes you win.

Track 8: "Lucy"

Written by: Mark Hudson and the Hanson brothers.

Lead singer: Zac, the Hanson who can really hit those high notes.

Tempo: Midtempo power ballad.

Dance/Clap-o-Meter: Another one to sway to. Score: 4.

Weep/Sap-o-Meter: It's no "Weird," but tears will roll. Score: 8.

Major theme: You don't know what you've got till it's gone.

What they say: So, who's Lucy? A girlfriend? Guess again. Comedy icon Lucille Ball (after all, the phrase "I Love Lucy" is repeated)? Nick at Night notwithstanding, uh-uh. Think Peanuts. As in the *cartoon* Lucy. Well, that's how it started. Mark Hudson picks it up: "There's a signed lithograph of the Schroeder and Lucy characters from the Peanuts cartoon strip in my studio. I was looking at it when the boys were there and suddenly pictured Zac's face instead of Schroeder's. I wanted to write a song for Zac—and that's how it came about. We all started grooving to the idea. I helped them with the lyrics, but they kept it all in their perspective."

Storyline: Oops, his bad. It's a heartbreak-kid tale of a boy who took a girl for granted, left her, and would now desperately do anything to rewind that tape. She was the devastated one at first, but she's doing okay now. He's not. The world as he knew it is over without her.

Who will relate: Anyone who's ever coped with loss and longing, and wished to take back the bad!

Track 9: "I Will Come to You"

Written by: The Hanson brothers, plus legendary composers Barry Mann and Cynthia Weil.

Lead singer: Taylor mostly, but he, Ike and Zac trade lines through much of it.

Tempo: Slow; a lean-on-me power ballad, it's the prom song on the album.

Dance/Clap-o-Meter: A romantic *slow* dance with a major sway factor. Score: 9.

Weep/Sap-o-Meter: Not weepy, but sappy. Score: 9.

Sing along-ability: Those "nah, nah, nah, nah, nahs" are going to be repeated ad infinitum.

Major theme: Like a bridge over troubled water, I will ease your way (apologies to Simon and Garfunkel).

What will happen: "I Will Come to You" is an instant classic; this is the one Hanson should end all their concerts with.

Storyline: Female Hanson fans will swoon to this knight in shining armor song. More a declaration than a story, it sounds like it's about a boy who vows unconditional love and support for the girl he loves. It doesn't matter how low she feels, how isolated and alone, she can always rely on him. Best of all, she doesn't even have to call, or even say anything. He loves her so deeply, knows her so well, he will hear her 'spirit' calling out to him—and he'll be there. But there's more than one level to this song. It's also about friendship, and loyalty, and true-blue buds intuitively knowing how the other is feeling, and always being there for each other—even if they're separated by distance.

Who will relate: Calling all romantics! On a fantasy girl-boy level, surely, everyone. But also anyone whose best friend moved away, who felt that "no one will ever understand me like she did."

Track 10: "A Minute Without You"

Written by: The Hanson brothers and Mark Hudson.

Lead singer: Isaac, with Taylor comin' in on the "Oh, yeah!"'s.

Tempo: A fun, swirling, upbeat rocker.

Dance/Clap-o-Meter: Oh, yeah. Score: 8.

Weep/Sap-o-Meter: Nah. It's just fun. Score: 1.

Major theme: Obsessive love.

What they say: "We had written just about all the song, but Mark Hudson finished it off," Taylor says. "This was their song," Mark Hudson agrees. "They brought it to me, only what they thought was the bridge was really the chorus. I tinkered with it musically—Ike and Taylor were cool with my changes, but at first Zac wasn't. He dropped his lower lip and said, 'I liked it the way it was.' So we worked on it a little more. The most important thing to me was that it be Isaac's song. Taylor's the lead singer, but it must never be forgotten that Isaac has a great voice. I wanted at least one song on the album to showcase that."

Storyline: This one's just pure, straight-ahead fun, reflecting the over-the-top feelings of a boy who feels so strongly, so passionately about his girlfriend that being separated from her for any length of time is a bummer. He feels like he just can't live without her, and how all time seems to drag on when they're not together. But there are no dark overtones here—as she apparently feels the same way. The fun is the speed-up chorus: Will fans keep up?

Who will relate: "All love is a form of obsession," goes the famous quote, and this track is for anyone who's ever felt that kind of joyful obsession for another.

Track 11: "Madeline"

Written by: The Hanson brothers and Cliff Magness.

Lead singer: Taylor and Isaac switch off.

Tempo: Midtempo.

Dance/Clap-o-Meter: Not a classic foot-stomper, but go ahead and try. Score: 6.

Weep/Sap-o-Meter: A heartbreak weeper. Score: 8.

Major theme: An on-again, off-again relationship.

What they don't say: Is there really a Madeline, or did they just use the name because it rhymed easily?

Storyline: A plaintive plea from a boy to the girl he loves. They're in a complicated relationship: They belong together, but they keep falling apart, making the same mistakes over and over again.

Who will relate: Anyone who's ever been in that kind of on-again, off-again relationship.

Track 12: "With You in Your Dreams"

Written by: Isaac, Taylor and Zachary Hanson.

Lead singer: Taylor. You can hear the struggle in his voice not to cry.

Tempo: A gospel-tinged piano ballad.

Dance/Clap-o-Meter: In the immortal words of

movie character Donnie Brasco, "Fuggeddaboudit!" In other words, score: 0.

Weep/Sap-o-Meter: Full-tilt sobfest. Score: 10.

Major theme: Love means never having to say goodbye.

What they say: "We wrote this for our grandmother, who died." In fact, the track, which is dedicated to grandmom Jane Nelson Lawyer, was written while she was dying, making it even more poignant.

Storyline: Got a tissue handy? Got several? "With You in Your Dreams" may have been written *for* their grandma, but it's written *from* her point of view: She knows she's dying, but she's telling the boys it's okay, that they must go on living their lives, remember the happy times, and always know she'll be there, their memories of her etched forever in their waking dreams.

Who will relate: Anyone who's ever lost a beloved relative or friend.

Bonus Track 13: "Man from Milwaukee" (Garage Band Mix)

Written by: The Hanson brothers, but they give Zac most of the credit.

Lead singer: Taylor.

Tempo: Bouncy, uptempo, fun, with the scratchy sounds of a walkie-talkie inserted here and there.

Dance/Clap-o-Meter: Go ahead, it's a joyful bopper. Score: 8.

Weep/Sap-o-Meter: No dark overtones here. Score: 0.

Quirk-o-Meter: Right, this one gets an extra category, being that it's an extra track and all. Score: 9.

Why it's called a Garage Band Mix: It's got a tinny, unpolished sound, just like it was recorded by an unproduced garage band.

Major theme: Zac meets a weird, wacky alien.

What Zac says: "I was in Albuquerque with my family when our van broke down. I was sitting at a bus stop waiting for my parents to fix it when this guy sat down next to me. I'd been thinking about aliens, and I suddenly thought, 'What if he's really an alien?' So I started writing this song. Only Albuquerque didn't have the right ring to it, so I changed it to Milwaukee."

Storyline: Sung in rhyming couplets, it's a Dr. Seuss like goofy romp about a weird, wild and wacky alien—with extra-large toes—who tells Zac about odd habits, like running around in his underwear and communicating with Mars. He uses a walkie-talkie, which is what Zac rhymed with—you got it—Milwaukee!

Who will relate: Your younger brother.

12

ON THE GIRLFRIEND TIP, THE FAN LINE AND THE FUTURE ZONE

"We're not looking for, nor do we have, girlfriends," says Taylor.

"We can date, but right now, a [potential] girl-friend wouldn't want to deal with it. It's definitely something we think about, but it's not a big issue," adds Ike.

"[Girlfriends] would see us about one minute a year!" explains Zac.

The Hanson hotties agree on most subjects: girl-friends, obviously, included. Even though this one *is* hard to believe. They're so cute, so talented, such sweeties. And they've been girl-magnets since they started singing together five years ago. Hooking up with, at the very least, a hometown honey would've seemed natural.

Why haven't they? Why aren't they looking? It's

simple: Ike, Taylor and Zac appear to have made an "executive decision" to put relationships on hold and dedicate themselves completely to their music and their career. Apparently it's not a new decision. As their mom told the manager of Big Splash Water Park back in 1995, "We don't do girlfriends. We have friends, but that's it."

Ike, Taylor and Zac seem to feel that having an exclusive relationship with someone right now just wouldn't be fair. To the girl, to themselves and—according to Taylor—to their fans.

"Fans don't like it," the Hanson in the middle explained candidly to *16* magazine. "It's pretty weird. You have a fan trying to get an autograph, and then you tell her you have a girlfriend, and it's like, 'Oh, bummer.'" Tay and the guys are clearly sensitive to their fans' feelings, so much so, they're willing to sacrifice romance for them. Which is either extremely cool or kind of weird, depending on your point of view.

Okay, but still.

Ike, Tay and even Zac *are* very hot; and one listen to their lyrics reminds you that they do think about girls, romance and love. A lot. And the no-girlfriends ban can't last forever. So what kind of girl would a Hanson look for if a Hanson would be looking? And what would each Hanson be like as a date? Which Hanson matches up best with you? They won't talk about it publicly, but check out their Love-o-Scopes: Here's what a fan can glean, astrologically speaking, on the Hanson dating scene.

WHAT IKE LIKES

"Ike's got girls on the brain," asserts Hanson family friend Jarrod Gollihare. Which, in light of Ike's own for-the-record comments (including this, to the L.A. press recently: "We don't want to get into the whole dating thing. It's about the music."), may be somewhat of an exaggeration, but still, it may not be *too* far off. For the sixteen-year-old Hanson does often crack witty about celebrating his success by "getting a hot date." And there is at least one rumor circulating on the Internet alleging that Isaac has a girlfriend. And according to Zac, Ike is the romantic type, "the one who'd dedicate songs to girls."

According to his astrological profile, that fits. Scorpio boys have had romance on their minds ever since they were kids. And if Ike follows a typical Scorpio pattern, he'd be a neat catch for the right girl. Scorpios are great listeners, they want to know all about you, and they really care what you think. They're brutally honest, though: They don't flatter falsely. So if you really want an opinion on that dress, better be prepared for the truth. Someone who bruises easily emotionally might find a Scorpio tough on the ego.

He's a leader, not a follower, and he would definitely have an opinion about what he wants to do on a date. There wouldn't be many "What do *you* want to do? I don't know, whatever *you* want to do" conversations. But he's reasonable, open to other ideas and opinions; a girl would definitely have to make hers known, however. Guessing games are not for him. His strongest characteristics are his honesty, his integrity, his courage.

The girl for Scorpio Ike is patient and strong-minded. She'd need to respect his decision to not interrupt his career for love; she'd earn his respect by following her own dream.

A Date with Taylor

Taylor may be the most sought-after Hanson, but according to him, he's not seeking. Not right now, anyway. Like his brothers, Tay's not cool answering girl and dating-related questions, but when pressed, he has politely allowed that "There's a whole world of hot chicks out there."

Typical Pisces princes are mega-romantic. They send flowers, remember birthdays and anniversaries. They're charmers with enchanting smiles and winning ways. Taylor's a totally trustworthy listener, the type of boy a girl could tell her deepest secrets to and be confident he'd never judge her harshly. Being nonjudgmental is the Piscean nature. So is his natural instinct to help. He's the compassionate one, the one with the outstretched arm to anyone in need.

A Pisces on a date is mega-easygoing: Wherever you want to go is usually fine with him. In fact, there are times when he needs someone else to light a fire under him to get going at all. Or to make the first move. A girl might find herself picking up the phone, doing the asking-out part.

And because he doesn't want to hurt anyone's feelings ever—nor would he want to fib—a Pisces is prone to dodging direct romantic questions. He'd say "maybe" when a simple "yes" or "no" might've been preferred.

His best qualities are his pure heart, his compassionate and altruistic nature. A girl for him could be a dynamic mover and shaker—but she'd have to be long on understanding too. And one more tip, from Tay himself: When asked if he'd date a girl who was a fan, he said, "Not if she was obsessed, but if she was nice enough, yeah."

Like Ike, Tay may be unavailable now, but he's worth the wait.

AND THEN THERE'S ZAC

"This girl came up to me and said, 'Will you go out with my little sister?' And I was like, 'I don't go out with girls yet. I'm not gonna get married in the next five or six years.'" On the one hand, the almost-twelve-year-old Hanson seems incredulous that someone would expect him to be dating; but this is Zac, remember. So it shouldn't be surprising that he's also said, "You can't avoid getting girls if you're a guy in a band!" And in answer to his idea of a perfect date, he sounds just like Ike when he responds, "A hot chick!"

That Zac has thought about his future on the dating scene is obvious—but what's also obvious is that he spends more time thinking about his music, his drawing, his Power Rangers, even aliens. No way is Zac close to ready to date, even if the Hanson no-girlfriends policy were suddenly to change tomorrow.

Zac doesn't lack for friends: He's got lots, both boys and girls. And he's a great, and way-energetic, friend to go out with. Like all Libra guys, he loves to have fun, and though he doesn't like to be rushed, he's the type to whiz from one activity to another. It wouldn't be unusual to hit a video arcade, amusement park, fast-food joint and a movie, all in the same day. Zac's friends have to be able to keep up with him.

He may not seem the romantic type, but it is a young Libra boy's nature to have many crushes. And underneath that joking nature, he's kindhearted and fair. He'd do anything to avoid hurting someone else's feelings. Typical Libras are big talkers—but they're also, once you get their attention, the best listeners.

The perfect friend for Libra Zac? She'd appreciate and roll with his life-of-the-party side, but she'd also be able to instinctively see the loving soul beneath it.

HANSON FANS RULE!

"The scream squad" is what Zac has tagged the legion of female fans on the band's Tulsa turf who've been on the Hanson tip for up to five years. "And it's cool to have people screaming at you," he adds.

"We do have groupies," Ike has admitted, somewhat sheepishly.

"It's cool to have people respond to you," Taylor tells us.

What's really cool is the way Hanson has responded to their fans. Which is with the utmost respect, and sincere gratitude. They're always gracious, always take all the time that's needed to talk to fans, give autographs, pose for photos. They did it back when they were playing elementary schools and water parks; they do it now. As Zac told *Rolling Stone* magazine, "There are more fans now, so it's more fun—just more!" Indeed, fans from all over the globe now recognize and often follow Hanson everywhere they go.

But do Hanson's Oklahoma fans have a hometown advantage? They probably used to: They've certainly demonstrated their worshipful devotion. Ike and Tay tell the story of one fan who showed up at their door unexpectedly.

"There was this one time we had a party, and all our friends had Nerf guns, and a fan came to the door. So we fired at the door, and she ran away. Later, we felt really bad about it, we figured she'd be really mad. But later, she called us up and actually thanked us for shooting at her!"

The brothers express surprise but no doubt, deep down, feel they dodged a bullet themselves. Hanson doesn't like losing fans, and being rude is a complete aberration, and very much against their nature.

So, however, is taking the fan adulation too seriously. The boys know that fans who profess to worship them don't really *know* them as individuals—just as the cute, hot group of the moment.

"All the screaming girls going crazy, you just have to have fun with it," Taylor says, "but it's really not about you. You're kinda holding a position." Then he adds playfully, "Hopefully, we'll get to hold that position for a while!"

Ike adds a dab of big brotherly wisdom: "You have to remember that this kind of [fame] can go just as fast as it can come—and for us, it's come really fast. So it can go just as fast."

Ike doesn't say it, but he might add: "in an MMMBop, in fact!"

WHERE DO THEY G(R)O(W) FROM HERE: THE FUTURE ZONE

The future of Hanson has been the subject of much debate—and not all of it has been positive. Cynics abound, especially in the media.

"Is Hanson on the tenure track, or one-hit wonderland?" asked *USA Today* of several experts. The answers they got were mixed. Most of the doubters and detractors point to Hanson's age and their upbeat songs as a detriment to longevity in the music world. Others point to the same two factors as the very reasons they *will* survive.

A reporter from the *Philadelphia Inquirer* said, "I think they have the musical talent to grow, but . . . so far, they've only proven they can do one thing. It's certainly working, but you can't go to this well more than a couple of times."

"Young fans outgrow bubblegum bands," answered a representative from *Hits* magazine. "However, if you look past the surface, [Hanson has] quality lyrics."

Not to mention good timing. "It's been a long time since we've had young bands doing really good things, not shlocky, sugary pop. Young fans need something fresh. There's only so much shoe-gazing grunge rock they can take," added the *Hits* writer.

"If record companies can find young talent like the Jackson 5 and nurture it, they can ride that wave for years," wrote an editor at the trade publication *Radio & Records,* who added that Hanson probably is the right band at the right time and will last. "Young audiences tend to be more passionate about music, and they tend to spend more on music."

The *Austin* (Texas) *American-Statesman* was less optimistic, and even less inclined to be kind. Comparing Hanson to other young newcomer musicians, the paper basically said, "We hope Hanson doesn't ruin [the chances of] legitimate bands like Radish and Jonny Lang."

E! Online had this to say: "They'll be okay if they can avoid the media freak show." In other words, the talent is there, but is the maturity not to get caught up in their own glowing press—or the adulation of their ever-growing fan base?

At least one friend of the family doesn't think it'll be a problem: "They're as sweet as can be. If anyone has a chance *not* to get corrupted by fame, they do."

Mark Hudson was once a third of a teen-idol brother group. He's been there, done that. While working on *Middle of Nowhere* with Hanson, he gave them a piece of advice. Two pieces, actually.

Mark reminded Ike, Tay and Zac that fame and fortune bring their share of tough stuff. "It isn't

always going to be rosy," he told them, "the screaming girls, the people shoving you to do this, do that,
pulling at you from all directions." And, as was his
own experience, it is tough should one brother get
more popular than the others. (In Mark's case, it was
Brett Hudson who drew the lion's share of attention.)

To cope, Mark offered this: "Support each other,
love each other, never forget why you got into this
and be there for each other. The best thing you guys
have is each other."

And: "Keep the focus on the music. Remember
that all the people you idolize, Steven Tyler, Alanis
Morissette, these people are your competition now.
You'll have to make really great music to keep up."

Hanson is more than capable of following both
those pieces of advice. Few brothers are closer; few
musicians are more determined to keep the focus on
the music.

Ike puts it this way. "We love to make music, we
love doing what we're doing. We love where we are,
and we want to keep doing it our entire lives. We're
just trying to learn more, and keep getting better at
our job. We all want to stay in the music biz. We
hope we'll be doing this for another twenty-five
years."

Of course, music might not be *all* Hanson is doing
a few years down the road. While they didn't seem
keen on Rosie O'Donnell's sitcom suggestion, Ike,
Tay and Zac do think about growing and expanding
their talents. "We're interested in lots of things,"
Taylor told *Teenbeat* magazine. "We'd like to pro-

duce music and movies, whatever inspires us. We might consider doing music for other artists. But obviously, we're always going to sing."

Ike is more direct: "We want to pursue the whole entertainment industry, because we're interested in doing movies."

Zac's the one with the backup plan—sort of. "I hope we get to stay in the music biz and maybe do some acting or directing films or something like that. Actually, I'd like to be a cartoonist if this doesn't work out. I don't want to be stuck behind a desk."

Whatever else they do, Ike believes they'd never give up music for it. They couldn't. "Music is a part of us. It's what we've always done and intend to be doing for a long time. If we weren't doing music, then we wouldn't be who we are. Music is our life. It's what we love."

Unsurprisingly, it's Zac with the knack for summing it all up: "We can't break up. We're brothers!"

Bonus Section!

How to Reach Hanson

Snail mail: P.O. Box 703136, Tulsa, OK 74170
The advantage of sending letters the old-fashioned way is that the band gets to see your handwriting, and you might get something tangible in return. The disadvantage is obvious: It's slo-o-o-w! However, Ike, Tay and Zac insist they do read the letters.

E-mail: hansonfans@hansonline.com
The boys check in with their E-mail as frequently as possible. Taylor told *Rolling Stone,* "We get both sides, the 'Oh, I hate you guys, you stink' side, and the 'You guys are so awesome' side. The positive outweighs the negative by far."

Phone mail: 918-446-3979
You can phone for a recorded message of updated Hanson info and possibly, if the mailbox isn't full (it

often is), leave your own message. Be aware: That's a toll call, and checking with Mom and Dad—or whoever pays the phone bill—is a must.

HANSON ON THE WEB

The Internet is, of course, a great place to interface with other Hanson fans and get the latest update on the band. There are dozens of sites to check out, including the official one. Here's that and another cool one. (FYI: The beginning of all Web sites is: **http://**)

www.hansonline.com is the band's official site. Recently overhauled, it will feature sounds and photos not available anywhere else.

www.hansonhitz.com is one of the best sites. It features download-able pix and sound-bites, transcripts of articles and interviews, lyrics, FAQs and chat rooms. The site has had over 200,000 hits already!

The best way to find all the other Hanson sites is by going through Yahoo! (start at Cool Links, then go to Entertainment, and then Music) or other search engines.

THE SECRETS NO ONE KNOWS: TRUE TRIVIA!

● Ike, Taylor and Zac carry a journal around with them wherever they go—not only in case a cool idea for a song comes up, but to record all their on-the-road experiences.

● They have no favorite songs on their album.

"We love all the songs," Zac exclaims. Ike adds, "You really get attached to all the songs in different ways because of how they came about, their individual meanings."

● Although it's been spelled many times, many ways . . . it's *MMMBop*. Why? Because they like it. "It just looked good," Ike says. "Three *Ms* looked like the right size. It wasn't quite *MmmmmmmBop* and it wasn't quite *MmBop*. It was *MMMBop*, a little bit in the middle. It just looked good, three *Ms* and a *Bop!*" It's pronounced *ooombop!*

● When "MMMBop" hit number one, it made music trivia history. According to the ChartBeat column in *Billboard*, it's the first time since June 1979 that a group comprised of three brothers has been on top. Can you guess the group? Time's up: The Bee Gees, with "Love You Inside Out."

● Another Bee Gee connection: The same week in May 1997, both groups hit the Top 200 chart with the top two debut albums of the week.

● "MMMBop" also made history by reaching number one in the U.S. and England simultaneously—the first debut song by any group ever to do that.

● The first time Hanson heard "MMMBop" on the radio they were just getting out of a van, hurrying to an interview. They jumped back in the van and cranked it up. "It was awesome! It was great!" captures their collective reaction.

● The Dust Brothers, who produced *Middle of Nowhere*, are most famous for their work on the

Grammy-winning album *Odelay,* by Beck. Little known fact: Beck's real last name is . . . Hansen! Yes, it is spelled differently, and no, there's no relation, but the coincidence is kinda cool all the same.

● More name-news: According to Zac, when they were known as the Hanson Brothers, "a lot of people got it wrong and called us the 'Handsome Brothers.'"

● Just before *Middle of Nowhere* came out, "The Hanson mom came in and took back all remaining stock of those two independent CDs the band put out," remembers a salesperson at Tulsa's Sound Warehouse. Apparently no one wanted there to be any confusion between those self-produced efforts and the newly polished major-label debut.

● Though they live in the middle of tornado territory, they claim to have no twister-phobias. "We've never been in one" is the reason.

● They're not, as they told Jenny McCarthy, big fans of children's TV character Barney.

● Does Hanson ever get nervous on the promotional merry-go-round? They say no—or if they are, they don't let it show. Taylor says, "Nah, if you get nervous, you don't act like the natural you."

● The inside cover of their second indie CD, *MMMBop,* features the boys' original drawings—it's a collector's item now!

● How hot is Hanson? Hot enough to appear in *Entertainment Weekly's* "Hot Sheet" humor column. The item went like this: "How young are the

MMMBop rockers? They can't wait till they're old enough to ask LeAnn Rimes for a date."

● One of Hanson's most devoted fans is shock-rocker Ozzie Osbourne's daughter. "She drives me crazy playing that bloody 'MMMBop' song," grouses the man who once made his reputation by grossing people out.

● Isaac told Taylor to blow his nose—on national TV! "It was running" is why.

● Taylor told Isaac that no one cares how he used to wear his hair—on national TV, after Ike was describing an old style.

FACTS AT YOUR FINGERTIPS!

Eye on Isaac

Real full name: Clarke Isaac Hanson.
Nickname: Ike.
Birthday: November 17, 1980.
Height: 5′8″.
Hair: Isaac's long locks are dark blond and tend to be frizzy. He often wears a tail.
Eyes: Brown.
Instrument: Guitar.
Favorites
    Music: Alanis Morissette, No Doubt, a lot of R 'n' B and "some country. I am from Oklahoma, after all!"
    Sport: Speed hockey, rollerblading.
    Color: Green.
Hidden talent: Impressions: Ike can do Kermit the

Frog and Bullwinkle, in addition to his Beavis and Butthead.

Best career advice he ever got (from his folks): "Music has to be the reason you're doing this. It can't be about the fame or the money or any of that stuff. You have to really love it."

Totally Temptin' Taylor

Real full name: Jordan Taylor Hanson.

Nickname: Tay.

Birthday: March 14, 1983.

Instruments: Keyboard, synthesizer, and bongos, conga.

Height: 5'6".

Hair: Blond. Taylor wears it shoulder-length, parted down the middle. Sometimes he'll clasp it back in a tail; if not, he tends to tuck it behind his ears.

Eyes: Blue.

Favorites

　Music: Counting Crows, Spin Doctors, Natalie Merchant. "I mean, just everything, all the Top 40 stuff and everything else, even rap."

　Sports: Soccer, basketball, rollerblading.

　Food: Pizza, McDonald's, mashed potatoes.

　Drink: Mineral water.

　Color: Red.

Quote: "Everything changes."

Hidden talent: He's an artist and does pen and ink or crayon portraits of people he likes.

Best career advice he ever got (from his folks): "You have to love music in order to do it."

His advice to wannabe rockers: "It's a lot of work; you have to really be dedicated. You have to really know what you want and keep goin' for it."

Weird Taylor tidbit: He uses the word "weird" possibly more than any other living being.

Fearless prediction: To close that too-cute gap in his top front teeth, Taylor may need braces someday—just like Ike.

Zac Attack!

Real full name: Zachary Walker Hanson.

Nickname: Zac (no *H*, no *K*)

Birthday: October 22, 1985.

Height: 5'3".

Hair: Blond, most often worn shoulder-length and free-flowing, but sometimes in braids; see the "MMMBop" video.

Eyes: Brown.

Instrument: Drums.

Favorites

  Music: Aerosmith.

  Food: Pizza.

  Sports: Rollerblading, basketball.

  Color: Blue.

  Video game: Laserquest.

Hidden talent: According to a Web posting, Zac can speak while belching!

About the Author

Jill Matthews is a freelance writer working in New York City. She has also written *The Lives and Loves of New Kids on the Block* for Pocket Books.